Father of the Bride

Visit our How To website at www.howto.co.uk

At www.howto.co.uk you can engage in conversation with our authors – all of whom have 'been there and done that' in their specialist fields. You can get access to special offers and additional content but most importantly you will be able to engage with, and become a part of, a wide and growing community of people just like yourself.

At www.howto.co.uk you'll be able to talk and share tips with people who have similar interests and are facing similar challenges in their lives. People who, just like you, have the desire to change their lives for the better – be it through moving to a new country, starting a new business, growing their own vegetables, or writing a novel.

At www.howto.co.uk you'll find the support and encouragement you need to help make your aspirations a reality.

You can go direct to www.father-of-the-bride-speech-and-duties.co.uk which is part of the main How To site.

How To Books strives to present authentic, inspiring, practical information in their books. Now, when you buy a title from **How To Books**, you get even more than just words on a page.

Father of the Bride

Speech and Duties

John Bowden

howtobooks

Published by How To Books Ltd
Spring Hill House, Spring Hill Road
Begbroke, Oxford OX5 1RX, United Kingdom
Tel: (01865) 375794, Fax: (01865) 379162

How To Books greatly reduce the carbon footprint of their books by
sourcing their typesetting and printing in the UK.

First edition 2008
Second edition 2010

British Library Cataloguing in Publication Data
A catalogue record for this book is available from the British Library

ISBN 978 1 84528 400 8

Cover design by Baseline Arts Ltd, Oxford
Produced for How To Books by Deer Park Productions, Tavistock
Typeset by Kestrel Data, Exeter, Devon
Printed and bound by Cromwell Press Group, Trowbridge, Wiltshire

NOTE: The material contained in this book is set out in good faith for
general guidance and no liability can be accepted for loss or expense
incurred as a result of relying in particular circumstances on statements
made in the book. Laws and regulations are complex and liable to change,
and readers should check the current position with the relevant authorities
before making personal arrangements.

For Alicia. The fragrance always remains in the hand that gives the rose.

Contents

Preface

Few of life's relationships compare to that of a father and daughter. From the first time he holds her in his arms to the day he lets her go, their bond is ever evolving. For some, the relationship is so profound, so close, so emotionally complex. For others, miles, mistakes and memories may sometimes have kept them apart. Like signals from a mobile, they've faded in and out, now strong, now weak, occasionally lost, but always ultimately restored.

Well it's happened. Your little girl has got engaged. What do you *really* feel about 'losing' her? How do react when your mature, sensible daughter regresses into a headstrong, unreasonable teenager? How do you deal with this new alpha male in your household?

Planning a wedding can be a bittersweet experience. What is ultimately the happiest time in her life – so far – can also be the most tense. The anticipation of starting a new life runs headlong into the chaos of wedding details, family feuds and financial stress. An emotional roller coaster ride has begun.

Weddings have come a long way since the first etiquette books were written. Words like 'divorce', 're-marriage' or 'single-parenting' were never even mentioned. The traditional average family of mum, dad and two or three children no longer exists, if it ever did. Today families come in such varied structures, that more and more couples are sensibly throwing etiquette to the wind and relying instead on their own common sense.

So where does the father of the bride fit into all of this? Anywhere you want, anywhere you're welcome, and anywhere it makes sense for you to. And that applies to the mother of the bride, as well. There are so many ways you can help, both emotionally and practically. You'll find that one of your responsibilities –

as important as walking your daughter down the aisle – is offering a shoulder to cry on. Another is to communicate with people, some of whom you may not have spoken to for years. Most importantly of all, you always need to be there to *support* her – in whatever ways she wants.

This will be is a momentous day for you, too. Acknowledge it. Never be afraid to express your heartfelt feelings, both privately and in your all-important speech. Why not grasp this golden opportunity to make a moving and memorable public tribute to your daughter (and her mum)? Don't hold back the urge to tell your daughter that you're so proud of the woman she's become and that you are truly delighted for her. She may already know it, but she needs to hear it from her dad.

It's not easy being a good father of the bride, but then again it's not easy being a good father. As you get older there are some memories that will stay with you forever – the first time your daughter uttered the word 'Dada', the first time you saw her in her wedding dress – and that precious moment when she said, 'Thanks, Dad. We couldn't have done it without you!'

John Bowden

Part One

Congratulations!

1 She's Engaged!

'My son is my son till he finds him a wife, but my daughter is my daughter the rest of her life.' (Dinah Maria Mulock Craik)

So your daughter is getting married. Does this momentous news fill you with delight or despair? Hopefully, you are truly ecstatic about the announcement. If you are, don't keep it to yourself. Tell the world how you feel. But maybe you're not quite so sure. If that's the case – and hard as it sounds – unless you have *very serious* concerns about his suitability, it's far better to hold your tongue. Let's face it, this wedding is almost certain to happen, whatever your views. So think long and hard before you say or do anything negative. How you react to the engagement will have a massive influence on your future relationship with your daughter. It will also help determine whether the run-up to the Big Day is going to be terrible, tolerable – or terrific!

Understandably though, for some fathers this can be an extremely difficult time. No way, she's just a baby! No matter how old she is, you can never quite get that vision of a smiling gap-toothed five year old out of your mind. You were the first man in her life, her first hero, her first love. You have sacred memories that still linger and refuse to disappear. The first day she toddled up to you and, for no reason, threw her arms around your neck. The morning the two of you stomped up and down in that mud pool. The afternoon you lay on your backs together, looking for shapes in the clouds.

Schooldays fly by. You're on a treadmill. You're her chauffeur, her financial backer, her best friend, her worst enemy. Then, before you know it, she's waxing her legs and wearing make-up. Things are moving quickly, too quickly, *far* too quickly. You begin to worry about the kind of man she might meet. You worry that he only wants one thing from her. And you know exactly what that one thing is because it is the same thing you wanted when you were his age.

Daddy, I've got something to tell you . . .

Then one day it happens: she tells you she's found a very special person. A new form of panic takes over. Now you're not worried that she's met the *wrong* kind of man, you're worried that she's met the *right* kind of man. In a cold sweat you begin to rationalise your fears. It will never last! He's totally wrong for her! Why does she want to be with *him*? But are your concerns genuine? Or is your fundamental fear that you will lose her? Your memory suddenly becomes highly selective. Didn't she once say she didn't believe in marriage? Didn't she tell you she was too independent ever to marry? Didn't she say her job and career would always come first?

Maybe she did. But people change, as do their priorities and passions in life. Perhaps she really has met the man who has changed everything for her. Maybe she's head-over-heels in love with someone she wants to spend the rest of her life with. Everything and everyone else has suddenly gone down her pecking order – and that includes you. Recognise that this is inevitable. She still loves you, but in a different way. If you play your cards right your relationship can become even stronger and more positive. If you blow it, things are likely to go downhill very rapidly. Don't make her choose between the two most important men in her life. If you do, you'll probably be awarded the silver medal – at best.

Thanks for the memory

Memories are wonderful. No one can ever take them away from you. But reality is something else. She isn't a kid anymore. Of course it's not easy; you're not only a dad, you're a man. You have feelings, opinions and concerns of your own. This may well be an incredibly difficult time for you but you simply must handle them – and handle them well. Whether you feel elated or whether the prospect turns your stomach, remember she's no longer that gap-toothed five year old, she's an adult. When it comes to questions of preference, the bottom line is that hers, not yours, must prevail.

Serious concerns, of course, are another matter altogether. Note the word *serious*. If he's 60 and she's 16, or if you've heard he's been bragging that he's only marrying to get hold of your daughter's money, then of course you have every justification in raising the issue. On the other hand, if you are concerned that he is not as eloquent as you might have wished, it is best to keep this thought to yourself. If you do decide to voice a serious concern, do so in a calm, rational, measured manner and at an appropriate time and place.

The role of the monarchy has been defined as three-fold: the right to be consulted, to advise, and to warn. You do not have the right to be consulted, but you do have the right – indeed the duty – to advise and warn, but always in a constructive and diplomatic way. She may dismiss your concerns as groundless. So be it. You can do no more. At the end of the day she has the right to be wrong. Come on, Dad, you knew this day would come. You have to let her go and hope and pray you've brought her up well. Your role now is to support, not to criticise.

How close are you to your daughter?

There is a direct causal relationship between how close you are to your daughter and how emotionally affected you are likely to be by the announcement of her engagement. For some fathers this is an incredibly difficult time. Emotions go into freefall. Other dads – and stepdads – are far more laid back. They have less of a problem accepting the situation. Maybe they haven't been on the scene that long, maybe they are no longer on the scene, or maybe they simply have never been that close to their daughter.

So how well do you know your daughter? What is her biggest fear, her proudest accomplishment, her favourite possession? And how protective or perhaps overprotective are you towards her? Do you sometimes worry unnecessarily about her? Do you feel she is not safe in today's world? Do you find it difficult to be apart from her? Or maybe it's the complete opposite. Do you live totally separate and independent lives?

In other words, your probable reaction to the news will be strongly influenced by whether the two of you have an honest and healthy relationship, whether you tend to wrap her up in cotton wool, or whether you are so wrapped up in your own life that you aren't at all concerned about hers.

What kind of father are you?

This is not asking whether you are generous or mean; strict or lenient; jovial or miserable. It is asking where you fit into sometimes quite complex family set-ups. For example, a child could have a natural father, a second father who brought her up, and a third father who is married to her mother.

Obviously, your relationship with your daughter will be affected by far more than just your 'status'. There is no reason to expect a biological father to get on any better with his daughter than a stepfather – or vice versa. However, potentially, each of these roles does present unique problems and opportunities which will now be explored.

You're a single dad

The relationship between a single father and his daughter can sometimes be highly problematic. Often they are either too close or too distant, too loving or too disinterested. And if their relationship is intense, it can suddenly swing from one extreme to the other for apparently the most trivial of reasons.

When a third party attempts to penetrate this love/hate relationship, sparks can really begin to fly. A once-adored father who finds a new girlfriend can create heartbreaking jealousy for his daughter. A dutiful daughter who finds a partner can cause agonising pain and resentment in her father.

If your relationship has managed to steer that tricky midway course between closeness and distance – if you are loving without ever being clinging – all may be well. Otherwise be prepared for a roller coaster ride of emotions – for both of you.

The fact remains that she has her own life to live and if she has now decided to marry, you need to support her. An extremely negative reaction from you could drive her away and destroy her chance of happiness. Mentally fast-forward 20 or 30 years. Let's face it, you may no longer be around and she may end up a lonely 50 or 60-something. Okay its cliché time, but you really won't be losing a daughter; you'll be gaining a son.

You're her stepfather

If the situation is proving to be difficult for you to handle, what must it be like for your stepdaughter? She may be horribly torn between her two fathers – or maybe she's concentrating on just one of you. However she decides to play it, you must go along with decisions and become involved in the precise way(s) she wants, no more and no less.

It may seem terribly unfair to you if you've been around for years and now she seems to be laughing, joking and arranging everything with a man who hasn't even sent her a birthday card since you came on the scene. Whatever you do, don't give her a guilt trip. Try to understand her motives. This is the man she spent her formative years with. This is the man she shares unique and precious childhood memories with. Children are the real victims of divorce. Perhaps this is her way of telling him: 'I don't blame you.' This does not mean she loves you any the less. On the contrary, it shows she knows how much she can trust and rely upon you. Support her decision and she'll love you even more.

On the other hand, she may have nominated you as the main man. Once again, go with the flow. Unless your wife's divorce was acrimonious and her ex did things that were totally unforgivable, with your wife's agreement, you could suggest to your daughter that she contacts him to get him involved in some way. Who knows, this could be precisely the approval she is secretly seeking. Believe me, if you make this magnanimous gesture, your daughter will shout your praises from the rooftops.

Three men and a baby

You may be neither the natural father nor the current partner of the mother of the bride. Nonetheless you were the man who helped bring her daughter up.

7

So where do you fit in this complex picture now? Yes, that's up to the bride. It is probable that she will treat you as her 'real' father and offer you the leading role.

If she doesn't, be aware that there have been – and are – other men in her life. Respect and support her extremely difficult decisions. If necessary, be willing to accept a co-starring or even a supporting role instead.

Etiquette and all that

As more and more couples have divorced parents, wedding traditions and etiquette are necessarily being modified or changed – or even being discarded by the wayside. Tell her not to worry about what used to be considered to be 'correct' or 'proper'; encourage her to do whatever makes her feel most comfortable. She may well confide that she has divided loyalties, that she wants both of her dads to be involved. However, she has no idea how this can be achieved. Suggest she divides the focus and responsibilities between the both of you. The invitations could include both of your families:

> Mr [Him] and his family and Mrs [Your wife] and her family would like to invite you to their daughter's wedding . . .

At the reception, perhaps her biological father could make the speech while you act as the anchorman, explaining who's who, giving a little background about the various speakers and generally keeping things moving along.

You're divorced from her mother

It is quite possible that your daughter will wish her stepfather to be included, possibly big time, in all the planning and parties over the next few months – and she wants to give him a prominent role on the Big Day. Perhaps you are fine with this; then again, perhaps you are not. Remind yourself that she may well have very strong feelings for her stepdad, especially if he has been an important part of her life since she was a child. Try to take a positive spin on things. Isn't it better for her that she gets on well with him rather than despises him? And remember: she could have excluded you altogether.

Daughters aren't all alike either

In the same way that your relationship with your daughter may be affected, to some extent at least, by your 'role' within the family unit, it may also be influenced by such factors as your daughter's background, current situation and hopes and expectations.

While the following observations may not be universally true, they should provide useful food for thought. They may also help you understand her – and your – complex and sometimes contradictory thought processes.

She's adopted

The fact that your daughter is adopted, generally, should be irrelevant. As far as you are concerned, she *is* your daughter. And, of course, she is. However, matters may become a little more delicate if she has made contact with her biological parents, or if one or more of them have got in contact with her. And if she was donor-conceived, then this can become a legal and ethical minefield which is well and truly outside the scope of this book. Suffice to say that your daughter should be allowed to make her own often very difficult decisions and that your role, as always, is to support, not to criticise.

She's had previous relationships

Perhaps some of her previous boyfriends have seemed a little odd to you. And maybe they have been. Remember that Elton John wannabe who wore a different pair of ridiculous spectacles each time he called? Then came that chap who spent most of his waking hours sleeping. And who could forget what's-his-name's impressive collection of giant African snails? Whatever your views about other men who have been in her life, you simply mustn't assume her fiancé is the latest in a list of oddballs. It isn't fair. And perhaps she needed to kiss a few frogs to find her prince.

On the other hand, maybe you think in the past she's let her perfect man get away. That was her (or possibly his or their) decision. Times have moved on. Don't pre-judge her husband-to-be or compare him with the one that got away. She wants to spend her life with him. Give him every chance to prove she's made the right choice.

You're anything but close

Not all father-daughter relationships are all sweetness and light. Yours may be a little cool, somewhat cold, or even downright freezing. Perhaps you haven't spoken for years. Then you get a call. What does she want? Cynically, you may think it's your money. Or maybe she really does want you around during this important time in her life. Be extremely careful: the way you react may affect your relationship for life.

You might consider yourself lucky. You have been given a second chance. However, don't expect too much too soon. You have bridges to build and that takes time. Respect her boundaries and allow her to dictate the pace to what *may* eventually lead to a reconciliation.

If you hear from someone else that she's getting married, it's fine to make a brief call, send a card or even text her. Acknowledge her good news and wish her well. However, don't expect she will automatically want you back in her life. She may respond positively to your conciliatory gesture, and then again she may not. Old wounds do not heal overnight. Let her decide how things may pan out over the next few months.

We've been here before

If your daughter has been engaged, and possibly married before – and may be more than once, it is hardly surprising if you are thinking: 'Here we go again.'

Hasn't she learnt anything from previous mistakes? Is she doing this on the rebound from that last 'big mistake'?

Maybe you are right. You are perfectly entitled to diplomatically raise any serious matters of concern, especially if history appears to be repeating itself. However, if you get the time-honoured 'It's *my* life!' response, make your case *once* and then accept the fact that she may or may not take your views and advice on board. Ultimately it is her choice. You have done your best. You can do no more.

Don't allow any personal bias to creep in

You also need to consider that maybe, just maybe this time she has got it right. Are you feeling the way you do because of *your* bad experiences? If you are divorced, you may be thinking, how can anyone of sound mind put themselves in a position to go through all the trauma I suffered? While this is an understandable reaction, it is not a helpful one. Second and subsequent marriages often work out brilliantly. And, in any case, it simply isn't fair to judge your daughter's decision unfavourably, based upon your attitudes and fears.

Daddy Cool

When it comes to paying for another wedding, whatever you do, do not rant and rave about all the money you have already wasted. That's history now. However, if you have previously forked out considerable sums, it would be unreasonable for your daughter to *expect* you to re-mortgage the family home to do it all over again. Of course, you may decide to do so anyway. That's up to you. But be aware that if you do not make *any* financial contribution, this may be interpreted as disapproval.

So unless you do disapprove, and you are willing to face whatever sanctions your daughter may deem appropriate, it is better to pay something, however modest. It is quite possible that she will take this as a gesture of your support – and at this stage your support may well be worth more to her than your cash.

You're *what*?

However you react to the news that she's pregnant, screaming and cursing won't solve the problem (if indeed it is a problem). If you feel let down, disappointed, embarrassed, try to talk to a person outside the situation. Perhaps you know someone who has already experienced something like this and has come through it well. To be able to help your daughter, it's important that you look after yourself as well.

If she has decided to keep the baby and feels this is the right time to get married, respect her decisions. She's probably confused, overwhelmed and uncertain what you think of her. You need to reassure her. Tell her and show her that you still love her.

It is for your daughter and her fiancé to decide upon the tone of the wedding. What do they feel most comfortable with? But however they may decide to play it, remember that a wedding should always be a happy occasion.

She already has children

Well, Granddad, you're going to have a (new) son-in-law . . . and possibly some stepsiblings, or even step-stepsiblings. Let's hope everyone gets on well. Children and young people are naturally extremely resilient and able to cope with quite difficult circumstances. However, if one or more of them is appearing uncharacteristically reserved, or being simply unwilling to talk about the wedding, or even acknowledge the existence of their stepfather or stepmother-to-be, there may be troubles ahead.

There isn't a great deal you can do about this, in the short-term at least. You can't call off the wedding; you can't allow only the 'best' of his offspring to join your daughter's family; you can't get a court order to take all your grandchildren into your personal care. Tempting as it may seem to you, don't tell your daughter that she hasn't brought up her children well, or that she's making a massive mistake in bringing new kids into her established family. If you overstep the mark you could easily drive her away from you.

It's a family affair

Hopefully though, for years both you and your daughter will have been helping your grandchildren become balanced, well-adjusted individuals. This will certainly minimise the potential trauma of the gathering of clans. If you haven't been as supportive as you could have, please start now. The following strategies really do help children face challenging situations, such as this one.

- Provide a safe, nurturing environment

- Spend time listening to and playing with them

- Teach them how to communicate

- Allow them to make mistakes

- Involve them in day-to-day activities and routines

- Trust and value them.

Let your grandchildren know you support them and that you'll always be there for them – if and when they want you. But never take *their* sides against *his* children. Let the extended family have no doubt that you care about everyone's wellbeing.

Is this my daughter?

Don't be surprised if your calm, mature, responsible daughter occasionally regresses to being a brattish teenager. The paradox is that this regression is actually in the service of independence. There is also an expectation that this time is supposed to be so happy, so wonderful. Yet in reality she will find it is fraught with ambivalence. Is it really surprising then if she loses the plot every now and then?

The process of getting married is rife with difficulties, as many issues collide during the socially sanctioned status of in-betweenness that is known as *the engagement*. During this concentrated period of time, it's perfectly natural for a bride-to-be to let off a little steam when the pressure of wedding planning gets too much. Try not to take this to heart. Normal service will be resumed – eventually.

Peer and media pressure

A decade ago, weddings were far less complicated affairs, largely due to the fact that couples did not have as many choices as they do today. Now there is a whole new wedding industry out all there geared up to pressurise your daughter to settle for nothing but the best. Each supplier will try to make her feel that the success of the wedding somehow rests on acquiring their most expensive product.

Images of celebrity weddings in newspapers and magazines have reinforced this message and a new condition, known as *Competitive Wedding Syndrome*, is sweeping the nation. A recent survey revealed that 59% of brides wanted guests to rate their wedding as the best they had ever attended, while only a romantic 26% wanted the occasion to show their friends and relatives how much in love they were.

We'll return to this syndrome – and how it can be treated – later. At this stage, just be aware that Bridezilla can be shown that it's the thought and personality that's put into the wedding, rather than the amount of the cash thrown at it, that will make her Big Day unique, personal and memorable.

2 Your Future Son-in-Law

'He's like you dad, except he's brilliant.' (Kimberley Williams in *Father of the Bride*)

There was a time – only a few generations ago – when it was traditional for every prospective son-in-law to pay a visit to his girlfriend's father to formally ask permission to marry.

Although this custom continues, it is not nearly as common as it once was. Today, when a man asks his girlfriend's father for her hand, he does so more out of respect than anything else. Generally, both the father and the boyfriend are aware that, approval or no approval, if they truly want to be married, there's little to stop them. The father's consent is almost expected.

Being asked for your permission

You've probably known your daughter's husband-to-be for some time. If he's been the only man in her life for years, the news couldn't have been that unexpected. But if things didn't seem to have been that serious – and you weren't given any clues that things had moved on so much – you may well have just thought of him as *the* boyfriend – or even *a* (current) boyfriend. In this eventuality, the engagement must have come as a bolt from the blue. And if you've only just met him – or even been made aware of his existence – then you were probably totally shell-shocked by their life-changing announcement.

Obviously it's easier if you've met before. However, even if you already know each other – and you've been getting on really well – this is a very different situation for both of you. You know it and he knows it. He realises he's now under a different kind of scrutiny.

Remind yourself that this man is probably extremely nervous. He could have taken the easy way out by leaving it to your daughter to break the news to you, by emailing or even texting you (not an uncommon practice today), or by simply not telling you at all. It is brave of him to speak to you face-to-face. Respect him for this.

Put yourself in his shoes

What did you feel like when you first met your wife's father? How did he treat you? How did you feel during and after that initial encounter? What lessons can you learn from your experiences all those years ago, now the roles are reversed? Don't make the same mistakes as *your* father-in-law.

Whatever the circumstances, the fact is your daughter has found the man she loves and wants to marry. However you feel about it, be careful not to say or do anything on the spur of the moment that you may later regret. And always follow the legal maxim: he's innocent until proved guilty.

Holding your tongue

Of course, if you know he's been doing unacceptable things behind your daughter's back, such as dealing in drugs, having an affair, being a serial fiancé who has already been engaged to – and then split up from – numerous other girls, you have every right and reason to confront him here and now.

In all other circumstances, hold your tongue. The time will come soon when it is appropriate to express your doubts, or at least ask some highly probing questions – but you should never do this in the heat of the moment. Be truthful: tell him you need some time to think about the situation and to talk with your daughter and wife.

Not making comparisons

Maybe you already have a wonderful son and/or a brilliant son-in-law. How can this man possibly emulate their exalted standards? The short answer is: he shouldn't be expected to. It simply isn't fair to compare people in this way. Everyone is different. Everyone has their own strengths – and weaknesses.

To you his weaknesses may already seem all too obvious. Don't dwell on them. In any case, there may be valid reasons or explanations for his apparent shortcomings. They may well reveal themselves over the weeks and months ahead. Don't jump to conclusions and give him plenty of time and opportunity to display his undoubted hidden strengths. Give him a chance. In fact, give him *every* chance.

Reserving judgement

If you make a snap judgement now, quite simply you may be wrong. Are you looking for problems with him rather than being open-minded? If so, how are you going to react when the nicer, more considerate side of his personality begins to shine through? Will you apologise? Will you keep up the pretence that you don't like him? Or will you tell everyone that you really liked him all the time? Even if you have doubts – unless they are major ones – it is far better to reserve judgment until you really get to know him.

Being consistent

It is perfectly understandable that in many ways you still see your daughter as your 'little girl'. But is it really fair to consider her in this way, yet to expect her fiancé to be a fully mature man? No, it isn't. True, he is not a child but he doesn't have the same life experiences and skills that you have acquired over the years. Speak to him in an adult manner, but do not expect the maturity of response that you would from a person of more advanced years.

Being open minded

Everyone has a past. By all means look for trends and patterns which could easily repeat themselves in the future. Is he giving you *excuses* or genuine *reasons* why things have not always gone as smoothly as he would have hoped? However, also be aware that people do change, mature and learn from their previous mistakes.

He's been married before

Perhaps he's been married before or he's been in a long-term relationship with someone other than your daughter. How do you handle that? Well first be reassured that this is a far from an unusual situation nowadays. You are perfectly entitled to ask him about how and why things have gone wrong before.

However, unless you are aware of any serious reasons for the breakdown of previous relationships, you should not form any instant judgements as to his suitability. Okay, he may have made mistakes and taken wrong decisions in the past (haven't we all?). Give him the benefit of the doubt. Sometimes it's difficult, but you really must give him every chance.

He's already got children

If he has children from one or more previous relationships, you are going to become an instant (step-)grandfather. However, you may feel about this, remember that your daughter has accepted – or even embraced – the situation. So should you.

His children may well already have one or two sets of grandparents. So precisely where will you fit in? Only time will tell. It's up to them, as well as to you. You may all hit it off brilliantly from Day One. Children certainly aren't limited to accepting love from blood relatives. And who knows, if you treat these children as part of your family, you may find you are seeing far more of your daughter and finding your relationship with her growing even stronger.

Taking it on the chin

Then again, things may not run so smoothly. Teenage children in particular can have massive hang-ups about re-marriages. If they don't like the situation – and even if they become verbally abusive to you – paradoxically, you really shouldn't take it personally. It is your role they are uncomfortable with, it's not you as a person. And never react in kind or expect them to accept you. In time they may come around – or they may not. Just let them know you will always be there for them, if and when they want you.

Of course his children may well be with their biological mother(s). Obviously your daughter should be made fully aware of any financial commitment your future son-in-law has to support them.

Love on the dole?

If he hasn't got a penny to his name, your first reaction will probably be: don't marry my daughter, or at least postpone the wedding until you can support *yourself.* Understandably, you would also have serious doubts if your daughter (and you) are well off and this impoverished person seems to have materialised out of nowhere.

But there may be genuine reasons for his hopefully temporary financial embarrassment. There is a big difference between a man who has just worked his way through university and another who has spent the last five years sitting at home, all day, everyday, sending off scripts to Hollywood film producers in the vague hope that one day one of them may be accepted.

Getting your priorities right

Perhaps he's never lived independently before and he's broke because nothing but the latest (and most expensive) iPod, iPhone, PSP, Nintendo Wii and DSi will do. If this is the case, he needs a serious reality check. Don't be aggressive, but point out that he should have other priorities in life, especially now he's intending to get married.

But he didn't even ask me

It is not unusual nowadays for a future son-in-law not to ask parental permission to marry their daughter. Don't take this as an affront. It almost certainly isn't. The world has moved on, and wedding etiquette is being dragged along behind it. Maybe he isn't even aware of the tradition of asking you for your daughter's hand. Or maybe he thinks this custom is inappropriate in the twenty-first century.

Perhaps it was your daughter's decision for him not to ask you. After all, she is not your property (or anyone else's for that matter). It could be that she thinks it is courtesy enough to *tell* you rather than *ask* you. And she may have a point, especially if the two of you have not been that close over the years. Maybe she proposed to him, in which case perhaps *she* should be asking *his* parents.

Knowing the score

The bottom line is that both your daughter and her fiancé are adults with inalienable human rights. To be blunt, if they decide to get married, what right have you to stop them? If you do withhold your blessing, one of four things may happen:

- They will call off the engagement

- They will postpone the wedding

- They will continue with their plans to get married

- They will still get married, but sooner than originally planned, possibly in a different location and without any family involvement.

Unless you can convince your daughter that her fiancé is a latter-day Jack the Ripper, it is highly unlikely that the engagement will be called-off. It is possible that they may agree on a postponement, especially if there is some financial incentive to do so. However, it is most likely that the wedding will go ahead, with or without your approval. So, unless you want to drive your daughter away (metaphorically and possibly literally), ultimately you must respect their decision, and do so with grace and humility.

Meeting the family

It's never easy to be the new kid on the block. Do you recall whether you were immediately welcomed into your wife's extended family with open arms? Or did the assimilation process take months, or even years?

While it may be tempting to try to fast track him into your family circle, it is preferable to allow things to develop at a slower, more natural pace. With the average length of engagements in Britain now running at around 21 months, there should be plenty of time for him to get to know everyone before the Big Day.

Don't overwhelm him. Gradually and subtly get him more and more involved in everyday family tasks ('Could you collect a parcel from the sorting office?') and introduce him to other members of your family ('Any chance of dropping this off at Jane's on your way home?').

Getting to know you

Maybe you already know your future son-in-law well. It seems he's been around forever and he's become an honorary member of your clan, almost by default. On the other hand, perhaps you've only just met him and a little male bonding would not go amiss.

If you share a hobby or an interest, this could be the obvious ice-breaker. Otherwise let your relationship develop naturally over time. It is important not to put any pressure on him to do things or go places he may not wish to. Maybe he's quite a reserved character (and/or maybe you are). Make it clear that he is very welcome to join you, but also that there is no expectation on your part that he does so.

The important thing over the next few months is that you get to know him as a *person*, not just as your future son-in-law. To misquote Humphrey Bogart: 'Who knows, this could be the start of a beautiful friendship.'

Part Two

Duties and Responsibilities

3 Being a Fab FOB

'There is a special place in heaven for the father who takes his daughter shopping.' (John Sinor)

So it's official – the decision has been made and the countdown has begun. The big question for you now is: What am I supposed to do? Well, traditionally the father of the bride had three major roles: to walk his daughter down the aisle, to make that dreaded speech – and to have deep pockets.

Today, things are a little more complex and there are now as many sets of father of the bride duties as there are weddings. In other words, there are no longer any hard and fast rules and you will simply be expected to do what your daughter wants. She may want you involved big time; she may want you to be there to offer help and advice as and when required; or she may simply not require much if any assistance from you. Your best approach is to let her know that you'll always be there for her – and that you want to help and support her practically, emotionally and possibly financially, as best you can.

As we shall consider in the following chapter, your role may also be influenced by the structure of your daughter's family. Perhaps you are her stepdad, divorced from her mother or a single father. According to the circumstances, your daughter may wish to divide traditional paternal wedding duties between you and another man who has been important in her life, or she may wish you to assume some additional duties traditionally associated with a bride's mother.

However your daughter decides to play it, you could well be asked to become fully or partially involved in many if not all the following tasks during the build up to the Big Day.

Meeting the groom's family

Traditionally, the groom's parents would call upon the bride's parents shortly after the engagement was announced. This does not always happen today. However, it is advisable that you meet up – or at least communicate in some way – and earlier rather than later, especially if it is to be a short engagement. Clearly this process will become more complex if you are divorced and/or the groom's parents are divorced, especially if there are new partners on the scene. That said, it really is important that there is meaningful contact between all the 'main players'.

Hopefully, you will all get on well and, with the agreement of your daughter and future son-in-law, you can soon be getting on with some serious wedding planning. You may even begin to develop a real friendship and perhaps meet them socially. That would be wonderful, on many levels. However, obviously this eventuality is far from certain and you should never 'push it', even if you believe you owe it to your daughter to do so.

Them and us?

You may feel you have absolutely nothing in common with these people. They are outgoing, you are reserved; they are townies, you are country folk; you are from diverse social backgrounds. But you are wrong. You *do* have something very important in common: your daughter and their son. Talk about *them*.

Even if you do not immediately hit it off, be aware that you will need to work together, for a while at least. After that you may only meet on the Big Day, at your daughter's home and at the occasional family get-together. So remain cordial. Who knows, they may not be as bad as you originally thought.

Funding the wedding?

The average cost of a wedding in Britain is now in the region of £21,000, although estimates do vary from survey to survey. In 2009, *Brides* magazine broke down the average costs throughout the UK (converted to descending order) as follows:

Item	Cost (£)
Honeymoon	3,788
Caterers	3,706
Reception venue	3,450
Engagement ring	1,913
Wedding venue	1,653
Wedding dress	1,180
Photography/video	911
Champagne/wine	771
Wedding rings	602
DJ/band	552
Flowers	516
Car hire	319
Attendants' outfits	303
Groom's gift	289
Groom's outfit	272
Cake	258
Stationery	244
Beauty	177
Lingerie	101
Head dress/veil	94
Attendants' gifts	88
Shoes	87
GRAND TOTAL	**21,274**

Whether your daughter's wedding is going to cost more, less or about the same as this, at an early stage it is essential to agree precisely who will be contributing to the wedding pot and who will be paying for what.

Traditional weddings

In the past, the bride's father was expected to shoulder the majority of the wedding costs. Tradition dictated that he paid for:

- Engagement and wedding newspaper announcements

- The dresses

- Outfits for the father and mother of the bride

- Flowers for the ceremony and reception

- The photographer

- Most of the transport

- The wedding stationery

- The reception and all its trimmings (the big one!).

The origins of this practice date back to a time when daughters were something you had to pay someone to take off your hands. Only 30 years ago it was still the norm for the bride's father to pay for almost everything. Today less than a fifth of couples rely entirely upon the bride's dad. The world has moved on and costs are now generally shared more equitably.

But what if you are expected to be one of those traditionally generous fathers, but you simply can't afford it? If your funds won't stretch to paying for the whole wedding, don't start mortgaging your soul just to give your little girl the day she's dreaming of. Tell her what you can afford and be prepared to stick to it.

Modern weddings

With the average age of first time brides and grooms rising over the last 30 years from 23 and 25, to 29 and 31 respectively, more and more engaged couples are now financially independent and are tending to finance at least a significant proportion of their own wedding costs. Here are some of the most common ways in which 21st century weddings are funded:

- The bride and groom pay for the wedding themselves

- The bride and groom may pay the majority of the costs with both families contributing towards elements that they'd like to help with, such as transport, the flowers or entertainment

- The costs are divided equally between the two families

- The two families offer to contribute a certain amount towards the wedding, to be spent as the bride (and groom) wish

- If either or both sets of parents are divorced, a compromise is found using a combination of options.

A recent survey suggests that some 64% of couples are now paying for everything themselves, with 31% relying on their parents (13% looking to both sets of parents, and 18% being entirely dependent upon the bride's family). The remaining 5% are funding their weddings using a variety of other inventive methods.

Talk to your daughter and her partner to establish how they wish to go about funding their wedding. They may well offer to take responsibility for some of the wedding costs, and the groom's family may also be willing to chip in. If anyone but you is footing the bills for certain items, make sure you keep track of who is supposed to be paying for what. It is also important to keep copies of all invoices, so any subsequent queries about outgoings can be easily and amicably resolved.

Competitive Wedding Syndrome

The move from traditional quiet weddings to grand, glitzy, opulent affairs is being fuelled by lavish celebrity bashes splashed across the covers of *OK!* and *Hello* magazines. Posh and Becks sat on matching thrones in a gothic castle, while Rooney and Coleen hired private jets for mates as they revelled in a £5 million Italian extravaganza.

And where the so-called celebs go, fans follow, along red carpets strewn with rose petals. Of course your daughter wants her day to be special; she wants her dream wedding. Yes, a *reasonable* budget certainly helps, but the best way to achieve this is to inject plenty of personality, originality and creativity, not necessarily plenty of cash.

Setting a budget

Once the total available spend has been established, the next big question to be answered is: Who will be responsible for budgeting and spending? Will contributors simply hand over set amounts to your daughter and allow her to spend them as she sees fit, or will they decide at the outset what they are going to pay for?

If your daughter has a good head for money, it is best for her to have the ultimate choice of how the money is spent. In this way, her fate is in her own hands and she has no one to blame but herself for any overspending on such and such or any underspending on something else.

Helping her to prioritise

None of us have a bottomless pit of money. It is therefore important for your daughter to decide what is most important to her. An influential 'economic law', known as the Pareto Principle, states that 80% of what is important is represented by 20% of what exists. For example, 80% of a country's wealth is likely to be held by 20% of its population and 80% of a company's profits may be generated by 20% of its customers.

But this law extends to far more than just economics. For example, 80% of the time we wear just 20% of our clothes, and we spend about 80% of our leisure time with only 20% of our friends. In the case of wedding budgeting and expenditure, the Pareto Principle can usefully be re-named the Parento Principle. This law tells parents that 80% of what is most important to their daughter will be represented by 20% of what is going to happen on her Big Day. If you can help her identify this key 20% – perhaps for her it is be the entertainment and the meal, or maybe it's the floral arrangements and the venue – then optimum use of financial resources can be achieved by targeting 80% of her overall budget at the 20% of the day that matters most to her.

Being helpful and supportive

Once again, your roles, duties and responsibilities will be dictated by your daughter's wishes. However, you should be forthcoming with offers of help (and know when to back off). Most brides-to-be would appreciate the following assistance.

Being there for her

Let her know that she can rely on you to provide emotional and practical support. Your role is to listen, to love and to provide a shoulder to cry on, 24/7. Remind her that the most important thing for the two of them is to make the wedding true to their personalities and not to try to please everyone else or to live up to other people's standards and expectations. Encourage them to do whatever makes *them* feel happy.

Be prepared to undertake both major and menial tasks. At times the most trivial of chores will assume mega importance: 'Oh no, who is going to blow up all those balloons?'

Keeping her calm

Another related role for a father of the bride is to act as a calming influence when things are getting on top of her. Reassure her that at times a little tension is inevitable. However, if she becomes really nasty, unpleasant and verbally abusive to you, just walk away. Never allow yourself to become her whipping boy. And don't be tempted to spend your way back into her good books. She probably already understands that 'money can't buy me love'. If she doesn't now, she will – someday.

Being a source of advice

Some people appreciate being given advice, others don't. You know your daughter's personality and temperament. Diplomatically step in when it's appropriate to offer a pearl or two of wisdom – but butt out when it isn't. The advice you may proffer is not necessarily restricted to aspects of wedding planning. You may wish to pass on some legal and financial information that would be of particular value to an engaged or recently married couple. We'll return to this in Chapter 6.

Being flexible and understanding

Your daughter may have some tricky decisions to make, especially if she is a member of a complex family network. Who should sit at the top table (indeed should there *be* a top table)? Who should walk her down the aisle? Who should make that speech? Try to understand her inevitable and unenviable difficulties and dilemmas and accept her ultimate decisions and compromises.

Liaising with the clergyman or registrar

Your daughter and future son-in-law will arrange a meeting with whoever is going to officiate. They may well appreciate your presence and input. While the officiator will do his or her best to accommodate their wishes, there will be rules, regulations and restrictions they must comply with. Perhaps some traditional wedding music won't be sanctioned if the ceremony isn't in a church; perhaps there are places and times when photography or videoing isn't permitted; maybe confetti isn't allowed. Don't worry if it isn't. Bubbles make a wonderful substitute for confetti. Kids of 2 to 92 will have a ball blowing bubbles from those little wedding-themed plastic pots and the photographer is sure to capture some wonderful expressions on their faces.

Checking out suppliers

Do you have any areas of expertise that could prove to be of value during the planning and procurement process? A popular role is that of chief wine and champagne tester whose onerous responsibility is to sample and shortlist the various beverages on offer (hopefully literally). Other potential assignments could include visiting reception sites, listening to musicians or DJs in action and comparing the styles of photographers and videographers.

Being a chauffeur

'So what's new?' I hear you ask. You may have donned the proverbial chauffeur's cap more times than you care to remember during her earlier years, but perhaps this practice has lapsed since she met her fiancé. During her engagement your daughter and her mum may well appreciate lifts to potential wedding sites, florists, dress shops and the like. You could even go shopping with them, if you are all comfortable with the idea.

Your services may later be in demand to pick up guests from railway, bus stations or airports, to transport them to hotels and ferry them from ceremony to reception.

Helping create the guest list

If you are not hosting the wedding, there isn't much you can do to influence the composition of the guest list, unless you are asked to make suggestions. However, if you are the official sponsor of the event, it seems reasonable for you at least to have your say. This is where things can become a little fraught, the dilemma being: while *you* may be paying, it is *their* wedding.

While some names on the list will probably be automatic choices, with a limited number of places available, a full and frank discussion may ensue as to who should be invited and who should not be. If you simply cannot agree, a possible compromise would be a four-way split. Your daughter, her fiancé, his parents and you and her mum each invite an equal number of guests.

But we <u>must</u> invite them!

Alternatively, your daughter could invite more people than originally anticipated. Mercenary, I know, but to keep within budget, the amount spent per head would then need to be reduced proportionately. After all, the cost of inviting 40 guests at £40 per head is the same as inviting 80 guests at £20 per head, or inviting 100 guests at £16 per head.

In practice, of course, if you switch roles from accountant to father for a moment, you will realise that every time you roll your eyes you are destroying a piece of your daughter's happiness. Ask yourself: Who should be placed higher in the pecking order, your daughter's friend or Aunty Wendy, with whom your only contact is an exchange of Christmas cards?

Small can be beautiful

Each invitee should feel part of a privileged group, not a faceless label on a mail merge. If you have 100 guests, each one is a measurable percent of the dynamic. As numbers multiply, conga lines get unwieldy, and individual personality is dispersed across the room rather than focused on the spotlight of energy around the bride and groom.

Often a big party separates into a series of smaller parties all happening in the same room. A limited guest list minimises anonymity, since no one is relegated to the fiefdom of a table a mile from the main action.

Providing information for invited guests

Once the guest list has been finalised, you could offer to organise and send invitations and information to guests. These could be simple cards or complete wedding packs, depending on personal preference and the style of the wedding. Typically, these would be posted some three months before the Big Day.

World Wide Wedding

You could even design – or arrange for someone else to create – a personalised wedding website. This is not an expensive option nowadays. Many of the major wedding information sites on the net now offer users facilities to put together their own pages of information which would include everything guests are likely to need to know – and probably a lot more.

Getting the seating plan right

Perhaps your daughter wants the traditional seating arrangement including a top table, comprising the bridal couple and immediate bridal party, with closer friends and relatives sitting at the closest tables. Or may be she would prefer people spread about with no obvious pecking order. The important thing for all of you is to think about who would enjoy conversing together, even if they don't (yet) know each other – and, equally importantly, who would most certainly *not* enjoy sitting together.

If you want to avoid hearing the likes of: 'I'm only on table 7, while *she's* on table 3', suggest she gives the tables names rather than numbers. Suitable names would be ones associated with theme of the reception (if there is one), or perhaps words for love in various languages.

Choosing a gift

Obviously the choice of gift(s) must be yours. However generous you may have already been with wedding costs and regardless of whether you have bought them a practical, material gift and possibly intend to help them out financially, you may wish to give the happy couple a more thoughtful and personal memento. The possibilities are endless. Here are just few ideas:

- A framed photograph or watercolour of the ceremony or reception site

- A unique vase, bowl or other artifact created especially for them by a local craftsperson

- Anything personalised, such as champagne flutes.

The perfect wedding memento is usually the result of a little creativity, legwork or googling, not necessarily a high price.

Four parties and a wedding

Any excuse for a party? The announcement of a wedding gives party animals the ideal opportunity to let their hair down. While there is really no limit to the number of events that can be organised before a wedding (the 'big one', of course, coming *after* the ceremony), there are often three pre-wedding get-togethers which you *may* be involved in. They are:

- The engagement party

- The stag do

- The rehearsal dinner.

As with most wedding-related etiquette, over recent years traditional hosting roles and responsibilities have blurred. Nowadays, a party may be hosted by your family, by the groom's family, by both families jointly, or perhaps by the happy couple themselves.

Arranging the engagement party

An engagement party can serve a number of useful purposes. It can be a great way of introducing both sets of parents to each other over an informal meal. It can be an opportunity to bring family, friends and colleagues together under the same roof. And if your family is well known for hosting parties, it can be a memorable way of announcing the engagement to an unsuspecting world.

Try not to go over the top with the engagement party; you want to ensure that the wedding day does not pale or fall flat in comparison to the party. Venue, food and entertainment should be tailored to your guests and their preferences. Caterers and organised entertainment will bump up the cost, but leave you with a lot less to do. Cost out the various options and choose the best solution that is within your budget and appropriate for the occasion.

Keeping everyone happy

Engagement parties invariably involve guests of different ages and varying backgrounds Regardless of the degree of formality, it is important to keep everyone involved and entertained throughout the proceedings. The more informal the do, the more activities – fun games, quizzes, re-enactment of the proposal – you may wish to include. As you plan the event, try to imagine what different guests would appreciate being laid on.

Making the announcement

If the happy couple can contain their excitement long enough to break the happy news at the party, then make that announcement the focal point of the evening. Choose a time when most of your guests have arrived, but before anyone has the opportunity to drink a little too much. Get something musical to herald the big moment. If there is a band, a roll on the drums would be perfect. Otherwise, a loud blast of something fitting on the CD should get people's attention.

Be prepared to say a few congratulatory, upbeat words. You don't need to say very much; keep your powder dry for the reception.

Throwing a surprise party

If nothing has yet been organised, or perhaps even discussed, you could take the bull by the horns and arrange a surprise do. For this to work, you will need a confederate, someone in on your cunning plan. One of you needs to get the happy couple to the party, while the other keeps the guests in order until they arrive. You will also need to ensure absolute secrecy. Visit your chosen venue and explain to them the nature of the party. If possible, book a private room where the guests can gather. Let the establishment know that you and the guests of honour will be arriving a little later than the main party.

Tell your daughter that, as an engagement gift, you have booked them a romantic table for two and that you will be pleased to act as chauffeur for the evening. When the three of you arrive, escort them into the hired room where they will be greeted by a chorus of 'Surprise! Surprise!' and with a shower of confetti and party noisemakers.

Attending the stag do?

You may well not be invited to this pre-wedding bash. After all it is an important right of passage that the groom is supposed to share with peers, not parents. However, if you are asked, think very carefully before you accept. How would you be likely to react to certain revelations and disclosures of a personal nature brought on by your future son-in-law's copious consumption of Cognac? If you could handle that – and if you are a recycled teenager at heart who still likes to let his hair down, even though he hasn't got any – you would probably have a great time with the lads. But if that's not really you, it's probably better to start thinking up a prior engagement.

Remembering the rehearsal dinner

It is becoming common practice for the main players to attend a rehearsal dinner after their final run though at the wedding site. This meal is usually booked in advance by the happy couple. The atmosphere should be very informal. Relax and enjoy yourself. However, prepare a few choice words in advance just in case you are called upon to make a short speech or propose a toast. This is a good time to invite the officiant to the reception. He or she may decline if they don't know the family well. However, at least you will have asked.

And finally . . .

Some couples budget for a final pre-wedding get-together of guests immediately after the rehearsal dinner, especially if their engagement party was a small, intimate family affair. Typically this would take place at some local nightspot. By this means, people from both families get to know each other before the reception. Instant recognition on the day avoids awkward and icy introductions and facilitates an easy transition from ceremony to revelry.

4 Family Matters

'You can choose your friends, but you can't choose your family.' (Proverb)

The traditional average family of mum, dad and 2.4 children no longer exists. Today families often come with a mum, dad, stepmum, stepdad, siblings, stepsiblings, and even step-stepsiblings. And at the same time, an ever increasing number of these families are scattering themselves all over the country – and often all over the world.

Given these sociological and demographic trends, weddings and wedding etiquette are necessarily changing. As families now come in such varied structures, more and more brides (and grooms) are wisely ignoring – or at least adapting – wedding etiquette, and relying instead on their common sense.

Happy families?

A wedding is an occasion which brings people together. The problem, of course, is that not everyone gets on that well. Some people love each other, others like each other, others tolerate each other and yet others despise each other. The greater the number of people involved in the wedding celebrations, the bumpier the journey is likely to be. Your daughter knows this – and so do you.

The good news is there is no need to worry about what used to be considered to be 'proper' or 'correct'. Encourage your daughter to arrange things in a way that makes her feel most comfortable, perhaps by including or modifying some traditions and rituals that appeal to her and by disregarding others which she considers irrelevant or inappropriate. She may also wish to include something new that will drag the ceremony into the twenty-first century. That's fine, too. Who knows, maybe it'll catch on. Tradition has to start somewhere.

Rules of engagement

Don't assume the wedding will heal old wounds. That's a big ask. In fact, often the opposite can be the case with old arguments resurfacing. If things are not handled sensibly and sensitively, relations could easily deteriorate over the next few months – making the Middle East look like a picnic. At times you may feel the need to call in a UN peacekeeping force.

So how do you stop people fighting (possibly literally)? Try to establish some basic and civilised ground rules with which everyone can agree:

- No raised voices
- No name calling
- Everyone has the right to be heard.

Other than that, all you can do is retain your dignity and be seen to be impartial. Above all, remain calm. If you can keep your head when all about you are losing theirs . . .

Dealing with your (former) family

If there are family tensions or even feuds, your daughter will be placed in the unenviable position of trying to keep everybody happy. Unfortunately, this may not always be possible. At times, you may feel disappointed or even hurt by her choices. Difficult as this may sound, try not to take it personally or to feel slighted. She has some very delicate balancing acts to perform.

By all means talk to her and look for solutions if any arrangements are making you feel particularly uncomfortable. But don't embarrass her or make her life even more difficult by expecting any 'special treatment'. Empathise and support her – and ultimately respect her decisions. She will thank you for this.

Your ex

If you get on reasonably well, the fact you will both be present at the wedding and reception should cause no problems whatsoever. However, if your parting of ways was acrimonious and all you now have in common is your daughter, things could be tricky. How will your former partner – and possibly her new partner and stepchildren, together with your former in-laws – fit into the grand scheme of things? The answer must be: in precisely the ways your daughter wants them to.

Whatever your feelings toward your former wife, keep them to yourself. Don't say a single word against her. Smile graciously and be courteous, unchallenging and magnanimous.

I'm not going if you are

This is the nightmare scenario. Try to *communicate* with your ex, even if you haven't done so for years. Explain that your daughter shouldn't be forced to choose which of you to invite - and which one not to. Her day will not be as happy if you're both not there to share it with her. This is but one day in your lives, but it is the first day of the rest of hers.

I'm not going if you're bringing her

This is another extremely difficult situation. Once again, *talk* to your former partner. Is a compromise possible? Perhaps the new lady in your life could just attend the reception. However, be aware that if you simply cannot agree, your daughter may decide to exclude your new partner from everything, especially if the two of them do not get on.

How you react to this, of course, only you can decide. But do not give a knee jerk reaction. If you haven't done so already, think it through extremely carefully and discuss the options open to you with your partner. Remember that it's your daughter's day and this unfortunate situation is not of her making.

I'm not sitting next to you

We're on much safer ground here. Divorced or separated parents do not have to sit together. If you really cannot stand each other, you can either both sit in the front row at the ceremony, but with other relatives between you, or you can sit in the row behind her. At the reception you can be seated at separate tables, each with your respective set of friends.

Mum's the word

As if your ex's very presence wasn't enough for you to bear, you may also face the double whammy of your daughter seemingly only being interested in *her*: 'Mummy said this . . .', 'Mummy did that . . .', Mummy, Mummy, Mummy! And isn't this the very same mummy who did the dirty on you all those years ago? How can your little girl be so gullible and insensitive?

The fact is that she is not trying to hurt you. However close you are to her, she wants her mother around at this important transitional stage in her life. The reasons for this may be both her emotional attachment to her mother and also the simple fact that she appreciates having someone around who seems genuinely interested in the design of her dress and the flavour of the cake. This is not a popularity contest between her parents. Try to understand what is going on in your daughter's head and don't react negatively to the situation. Mum's the word.

You ex's new husband

The way you feel about her partner clearly will be influenced by the circumstances under which they got together. If he was the one who caused you to split up with your wife, it is hardly surprising if he is not at the top of your Christmas card list. However, if he met your ex several years after you amicably went your separate ways, your feelings toward him may be far more neutral. Either way, remember that your daughter should not be made to feel like piggy in the middle. She may well have found it difficult to cope with *your* divorce; don't make it difficult for her to cope with *her* wedding.

If the two of you get on reasonably well, or at least can co-exist without causing a scene, your daughter will be delighted. She may well ask you to share the traditional father of the bride duties with her stepfather. That would be an excellent compromise. However, if she wants her stepdad to act as the sole father of the bride, so be it. Remain dignified, charming and witty throughout and the guests will appreciate how well you will have handled and reacted to a tricky situation.

Your former in-laws

Once again, your relationship with your ex's family will largely be affected by possibly differing perceptions of what 'went wrong'. In their eyes, you may have been Mr Nasty; while to you it is obvious that you were (almost) blameless.

Whatever the cause(s) of the break up, it certainly was not your daughter's fault and, in any case, this is not the time for yet more recriminations. In an ideal world, of course, everyone would allow bygones to be bygones – for one day, at least. However, this is not an ideal world. Smile, nod and make small talk, if you feel able. But don't say anything contentious. And don't rise to the bait if anyone says anything contentious to you.

Your new wife

How well do the two most important women in your life get on? The fact that you love them both does *not* mean they necessarily love each other. If your daughter has 'taken sides', your new wife could either have pride of place, or could be horribly snubbed. Unless there have been issues such as physical, mental or sexual abuse, children usually want their parents to get back together and, as they see it, for happy families to be restored. Probably highly simplistically or even simply incorrectly, your daughter may have always seen your new partner as the only obstacle to the two of you doing just that.

You can't make your daughter love her new stepmum, or even like her. However, unless your new partner has unquestionably and exclusively been responsible for some serious issues and problems that have directly or indirectly affected your daughter, it is not unreasonable to expect your daughter to at least *respect* your wife.

Your ex has vetoed her presence

As we have seen, your ex may have said she wouldn't attend if your new partner does. This presents a horrible dilemma for you. You could simply walk away. But if you do, it may not be for just one day; you may be walking out of your daughter's life. It's a difficult call to make. Isn't it a pity how some separated parents do not realise that the only thing they now have in common is their daughter, and they are not willing to go some way to make up for the sorrow they caused her when they got divorced?

Remembering the children

Children of all ages can be deeply affected by marriages and re-marriages. However complex or difficult your personal situation, do not say or do anything without firstly carefully considering how it may be perceived by *all* the children in your family network.

Your other children

While your attention is understandably focused upon your daughter, it is all too easy to ignore or neglect the feelings of your other children. What do they think about things, both individually and collectively? Siblings obviously can love each other, but they can also be highly jealous and envious of one another. When these emotions co-exist, as they may well do now, this can cause an emotional maelstrom.

It's not fair . . .

A younger child may feel aggrieved that you appear to be treating her sister as an adult while you are always treating her as a child: 'She's only 18 months older than me!' Does she have a point? Some fathers tend to see and treat their older children as mature adults and their younger ones as mere babies.

Perhaps one of your children has been living with a partner for some time. He hasn't received any financial help from you but now he sees you being incredibly generous to your prodigal daughter. Or may be when he got married he had to pay most of the expenses himself because his wife's parents (and his) did not contribute. Why should his sister (and her fiancé) not have to make the same financial sacrifices as he did?

Money, money, money

Then again, maybe your financial situation has improved significantly since your first daughter got married. It had to be quite a modest affair. What must she be thinking now her sister seems to be being treated like royalty? Is she thinking you have done the best you could for both of them at the times, or is she resentful: 'He's always liked her more than me.'

Another potential dilemma can occur if one of your children has recently split up from a long-term partner and is feeling that her world has come to an end. How can you square the circle of appearing so happy for one daughter at the very time another is feeling so low?

Of course, there are ways to mollify if not totally satisfy disgruntled siblings. Perhaps a little cash or a gift might do the trick? Or maybe an understanding word is all that is required? That is up to you. The point is that you must remain aware that your daughter is not getting married in a vacuum.

Your stepchildren

It is possible that there may be long-running antagonism between your 'natural' children and your stepchildren. And if the wedding is to be quite a small affair, your daughter may wish to invite more friends at the expense of her stepsiblings. 'They wouldn't come, anyway', she argues.

However, if you want your stepchildren to be there (or at least to have been given the opportunity to be there), you should say so. Ultimately, money talks and, if you are paying, you could insist. Yet it is far preferable to convince your daughter that inviting her stepbrother(s) and/or stepsister(s) is the right thing to do. If she still wants to invite more friends, that's fine. She will simply have to cut back on some other area of the budget.

The happy couple's

When one or both partners already have children, it is essential for the children's viewpoint to be taken fully into account. It is not always easy constructing a 'ready made' family and the more thoughtful and understanding your daughter and son-in-law can be in considering the happiness of the children, then the greater the chance of creating a warm and loving family for everyone. It is worth remembering that marriage is all about families and with a little thought, this wedding could provide wondrous childhood memories for their children.

Once you are made aware of the engagement, tactfully advise the happy couple that the children should hear of the marriage from them and should be given time to get used to the idea before it is made public. Encourage them to listen to their children and to talk to them about the changes that will affect them when they have a new stepmother or stepfather.

You can help, too. Children can get some very strange ideas into their heads. One young boy thought moving in with a new stepdad meant leaving all the furniture and – far more importantly to him – all his toys behind in the old flat. Support your daughter by reinforcing her positive messages and by making sure the children understand and feel secure with the new arrangements.

Getting them involved

The very idea of the wedding itself may be traumatic for the children of the bride or groom. It is their life that is changing as well as their parents', the difference being that the adults have chosen for themselves whereas the children are often just expected to fit in. Encourage your daughter to draw the children into the wedding plans. Make them feel they too have played a part in the decision making process. And get them involved on the day itself.

- The wedding invitations could include the children's names, or even come solely from them

- Separate invitations from the children could be sent to their own friends and young relatives

- They could have their own miniature cake which they could ceremoniously cut at the same time their parents cut theirs. They would then be given the responsibility of handing it around to the younger guests

- Alternatively or additionally, they could have their own 'reception'

- Older children could be invited to take part in the ceremony by giving a reading, making a speech or proposing a toast

- Sons and daughters can act as best man, ushers, bridesmaids or flower girls

- The bride could be escorted down the aisle by her child or children, who could 'give her away'. (This option would also resolve your daughter's possible dilemma about 'which father' should do the honours)

- A carefully chosen present from a new stepparent may be helpful. A little bribery can works wonders.

Children need to see that the marriage is being entered into enthusiastically by both partners and the fun of planning (yes, it can be fun!) can lead to a united family feeling before the great day arrives. When there are children involved, it should be a genuine 'family' wedding, not one just for the bride and groom.

5 Money Saving Strategies

'A cynic is a person who knows the price of everything and the value of nothing.' (Oscar Wilde)

However large or small the overall budget, and regardless of who's paying for what, it's foolish not to always seek best value for money. Whether you will be picking up the tab for the entire shindig, paying for some part of it, or have no financial commitment whatsoever, you are sure to find some useful tips and advice in this chapter which you can use or pass on to others.

Weddings are notoriously expensive. Average costs in the UK vary from survey to survey. However, an average of averages suggests the current outlay to be in the region of a gigantic £21,000 – a 100% increase over the last ten years. Yet there is a clear distinction between the cost of a wedding and the cost of a marriage. In England and Wales, you can marry at a Register Office for around £100. So how can you save on, or make better use of that other £20,900?

There are plenty of articles and blogs out there telling you how to cut wedding costs. Unfortunately, they are all so extreme: either describing millionaire bashes, or worse, relating smug tales from people who got married for tuppence.

Finding the middle ground

Yes, we all know a wedding can be done on an absolute shoestring, but that doesn't help the vast majority of engaged couples who don't want to have the cheapest wedding in the world. Most people *want* to splash out a little while still getting a good deal. Of course it costs more to get married at a lovely country house followed by a lavish five-course dinner than to have a registry office ceremony followed by a pint in a pub. But there can be a happy medium.

General advice

The wedding industry is a highly lucrative business. Brides are continually being bombarded with ideas to make their weddings more fun, more competitive – and more expensive. With all this hype it's all too easy for even the most level headed person to get drawn in: that very same girl who was never the slightest bit interested in a donkey ride on the beach will now settle for nothing less than travelling like a princess in a horse-drawn carriage. While it is perfectly understandable that a bride will want to create a wonderful and unforgettable event, no one should have to take out a second mortgage to help her achieve it.

So the first thing to do is to agree a realistic budget with everyone who will be contributing financially. Then decide whether certain amounts should be allocated to various items of expenditure – such as catering, transport and entertainment – or perhaps whether the bride (and groom) should be in control of the entire pot.

You will never underspend

In the same way that Parkinson's Law tells us that work expands to fill the time available, so Father of the Bride's Law, in short FOB's Law tells us that wedding expenditure will expand to fill the funds available – and can often exceed them. When was the last time you heard a newlywed ask: 'What are we going to do with the unspent cash?' Therefore, be aware that, once disclosed, your established budget will be the *minimum* spend.

Neither a lender nor a borrower be?

When it comes to weddings at least, Polonius may have got this one wrong. Many people will say never borrow. True, we are living through a period of credit crunch where loans are far more difficult and expensive to obtain. However, whoever is funding the event may decide it is so important to your daughter that they are willing to take out a loan. That's a personal choice. What undoubtedly would be foolish would be for anyone to get financially crippled as a result of the wedding.

Employing a wedding co-ordinator?

The average UK bride spends 250 hours organising her wedding. That's equal to six full-time working weeks. If you and your daughter have hectic work schedules, or if she's getting married at a distance or just finds wedding planning too stressful, a wedding consultant could be the answer to everyone's prayers.

Wedding co-ordinators operate at a variety of levels and fees. Nowadays, many wedding packages include advice and support from a co-ordinator as standard. Start-to-finish consultants handle absolutely every aspect of the wedding, but at a price. Others provide an array of services, which might be billed at an hourly rate or a fixed flat fee per service provided. This gives you the opportunity of choosing precisely where and when you need assistance.

A popular alternative is hiring a co-ordinator to manage events on the wedding day. The co-ordinator ensures everybody is in the right place at the right time, checks out the reception venue in advance to make sure everything is perfect, co-ordinates serving, pouring, toasting and cutting the cake and pays the bills, leaving you and your family to relax and enjoy the day. A cheaper 'just for the day' option could be to hire a professional toastmaster. He or she would fulfil similar roles, although they would probably not pay any bills on your behalf.

Hiring a wedding consultant might seem like an extravagant extra, but it could be the best investment you make. Their services can be secured for as little as £500, depending on the size of the wedding and your specific requirements. They can often save you as much as this, if not more, by negotiating discounts with suppliers.

As always, personal recommendation counts for so much. It is essential to feel comfortable with the person you choose. A wedding consultant is a creative partner who should be able and willing to offer advice and opinions, in addition to looking after all the practical arrangements.

Visiting bridal shows and wedding fairs

This provides a great opportunity to see lots of different suppliers at one time rather than travelling to see different people around the country. While it may be rash to place orders on the day, you could ask them whether they would be willing to offer discounts if you were to order within a certain period following your visit.

Considering an off-peak wedding

A Friday winter wedding would be a lot cheaper than a Saturday summer do. Marrying late in the day makes it possible for the traditional wedding breakfast to be replaced by a more economical buffet and disco. If it's to be a civil ceremony, having the service and the reception at the same location cuts down travel costs and may well attract a discount.

Marrying abroad?

An estimated 30,000 British couples marry abroad every year. For these daring romantics, a wedding away is a quicker, easier and undoubtedly cheaper alternative to a big bash at home. They spend around £15,000 less than traditional, stay-at-home couples, forking out a more affordable £6,000 on a combined wedding and honeymoon.

You can find information on legal requirements for various destinations abroad at weddings.co.uk.

Roping in friends and relatives

Do you have a friend who is a DJ or a musician, an aunt who is an expert cake maker, an uncle who owns a vintage car? Try to make use of friends' and relatives' skills and possessions. Ask them for their help in lieu of a wedding present. Most people will be pleased to get involved.

Shopping around and haggling

Start early. Shop round and compare notes. As a rule of thumb: always get at least three quotes. Don't be frightened to haggle (or get someone to do it for you, if you're not comfortable with that). After all, they will have haggled with *their* suppliers. If you have received a lower quote for the same product or service elsewhere, play them off against each other. At a regular auction, the *highest* bidder wins the spoils. This is a Dutch auction where, all other things being equal, the *lowest* bidder gets your trade.

Googling

Search the internet thoroughly and you can save a lot of time and money. The World Wide Web provides information and resources for making purchases online. Many wedding websites provide links to wedding-related businesses that could be your answer to quality products and services at a reasonable price.

Don't forget good old eBay. It's a huge and very competitive marketplace. You may well find some great deals.

And in conclusion . . .

So there we have it. When it comes to funding a wedding, having a reasonable budget obviously helps. However, there are also huge savings to be made if you are prepared to shop around and do a little homework. It's a question of getting the balance right – or rather, getting *your* balance right. This is a massive day in your daughter's life and you certainly don't want to be remembered as the Scrooge who ruined it for her. But really it's the thought and personality that's put into a wedding – rather than the number and size of cheques thrown at it – that can make the event unique and memorable.

6 Offering Useful Advice

'I have found the best way to give advice to your children is to find out what they want to do and then advise them to do it.'
(US President Harry S. Truman)

As father of the bride, you may wish to pass on some words of wisdom, some exclusively to your daughter, and some to both her and her partner. Whether they wish to hear them, of course, is another matter. Only you will know if and when it is appropriate to make a few little suggestions.

There follows some legal and financial information and advice likely to be of value to people who are about to marry. These sections are intended to be broad in nature. **An important disclaimer: People should always take appropriate legal or financial advice before embarking on any course of action.**

Legal advice

Marriage is a contract with specific legal requirements which arise from that contract and affect the rights and duties of the parties and their legal relationship with third parties, including any children they may have. It is important that your daughter and future son-in-law understand this, are aware of the legal formalities involved in getting married, and are mindful of other existing legislation which potentially may be relevant to them.

The engagement

Since 1970, engagement has not been a legally binding contract so parties cannot sue for damages if it is broken off. There is usually no legal duty to return the ring.

Pre-nuptial agreements

A pre-nuptial agreement (pre-nup) is a written contract entered into by two parties who are about to marry with the intention of setting out their respective financial intentions and obligations in the event of a subsequent divorce. Since a landmark judgement in 2009, pre-nups can now be decisive when settling divorce cases.

Lawyers say the increasing number of independently wealthy women, coupled with greater numbers of people marrying later in life with complicated family arrangements, has increased their popularity.

Grown ups can now agree in the best of times what would happen in the worst of times. Raising this matter while deciding guest lists and honeymoon destination is far from romantic but, realistically, it *could* save a lot of time, hassle – and money – in the future.

Where can they get married?

The choice of venue is dependent upon part of the United Kingdom in which the wedding is to take place, as follows:

England and Wales

Under the Marriage Act 1994, which came into effect the following year, a marriage may be held in a place of religious worship, register office or public premises officially registered for marriages by the Registrar General for England and Wales. Civil marriages may now therefore occur in *seemly and dignified venues*, such as stately homes, civic buildings or hotels (but not open-air venues) which have been officially registered for the purpose.

In 2008, a new law, known as the Church of England Marriage Measure, came into effect. It is now possible for couples to have their wedding service in a church where they have a family or special connection. These 'qualifying connections' are:

- One of them was baptised or prepared for confirmation in the parish

- One of them has lived in the parish or regularly attended public worship there for at least six months

- One of their parents has lived in the parish or regularly attended church services there for six months or more in their child's lifetime

- One of their parents or grandparents was married in the parish.

Scotland

In Scotland, because it is the minister, priest, celebrant or clergyman who carries a licence, in theory, a religious ceremony can be performed almost anywhere, either in or out-of-doors. It should be mentioned though that different churches and individual clergymen may have their own views on:

- marrying couples who are from outside their parish

- performing wedding ceremonies in locations other than in their church.

Couples should contact the minister concerned to ensure that he or she would be willing to carry out the ceremony should either of the above points be relevant.

Northern Ireland

There is less choice about where couples may marry in Northern Ireland, as it was excluded from the Marriage Act 1994 which allowed venues authorised by the local authority to be used for weddings.

Are there specific days when they aren't allowed to wed?

Legally, civil wedding ceremonies can take place between 8am–6pm on any day, excluding Christmas, Boxing and New Years Day. However, registrars in different county council boroughs will have different rules and regulations of their own, so your daughter would be wise to contact her local register office to double check.

Getting married abroad

If they wish to marry abroad according to the laws of that country, then they will need to find out about the regulations that apply. To marry in another country often involves a minimum period of residency. Most countries will require couples to produce some kind of documentary evidence. To find out the requirements they should contact one of the following:

- the relevant embassy or high commission in this country

- the relevant register office where you wish to have your wedding

- the Marriage Abroad Section at the Foreign and Commonwealth Office in London (tel 020 7270 1500).

If they are informed that certificates of no impediment are required then they will need to contact the Register Office in whose district they reside to arrange to give their notice of intention to marry.

Whilst the vast majority of marriages that take place abroad are recognised as valid in this country, they cannot be registered in the United Kingdom. In certain circumstances, however, it may be possible for the certificate issued by the overseas marriage authority to be lodged with the General Register Office. This would enable them to issue a certified copy of the document at some time in the future, if required. Further advice can be obtained from the General Register Office (tel 0151 471 4801).

Same-sex 'marriages'

Same-sex couples are now able to enter into a civil partnership by registering a formal commitment to one another. This gives them legal recognition for their relationship, which means they have almost exactly the same rights and responsibilities as married couples.

Legally, does she have to change her name?

No. There is no official requirement for a woman to change her surname, but if she wants to take her husband's name, she is legally entitled to do so. Using the same surname as her husband is traditionally the easiest option for women, especially when children are involved.

Alternatively, her husband could change his surname to hers, by deed poll. A modern alternative is to make the new surname double-barrelled. Again for this, they would both need to arrange this to be done by deed poll. Established business women tend to prefer to keep their existing surnames. She could keep her original surname for work, and use her husband's surname for personal life. Really, she has the freedom to decide which is most appropriate for herself and her husband.

If your daughter is taking her husband's name she doesn't need to do anything after the marriage apart from informing the appropriate government departments, banks, and other such organisations she has dealings with. They will usually require sight of the original marriage certificate, or a certified copy of it.

The one document she can change *before* her marriage is her passport. This allows her to go on the honeymoon with her married name, but it's also fine to travel under her maiden name and change her passport later. If she needs to arrange any visas before her honeymoon, it might be wise not to change her passport until *after* the honeymoon as they may need to match.

Financial advice

Getting married is an exciting and meaningful stage in any relationship. But often, in all the excitement and planning, money and financial issues can get lost, buried or simply ignored. Managing money in a partnership is critically important and careful control of it will help both partners cope through many situations and potential problems.

Brides-to-be would often rather give themselves a beauty makeover than a financial one. But couples need their heads firmly screwed on and should take a long, hard look at their finances as they enter marriage.

Preparing finances for the wedding

When people plan to get married there are so many things they have to begin thinking about in the plural rather than the singular. Money is a key issue in this category. Here are some suggestions that should help:

Starting to save

Unless they are planning a very long engagement, most analysts agree that instant access savings accounts are the best place for their wedding fund. This is because, with plenty of bills to settle during the build up to the Big Day, they'll need to be sure funds are available when they need them.

Getting their finances in shape

Opening a joint account to cover essentials, in addition to retaining their own separate accounts, is an excellent way of dealing with combined finances. However, one of the greatest causes of unrest is the use of a joint account for personal expenditure. If one of them has a passion for Harrods whilst the other prefers Oxfam, it would be sensible for each of them to use their own current accounts for 'non-joint' expenditure such as clothes, hobbies and all 'frivolous' purchases.

Wiping the slate clean

They should make every effort to disentangle themselves from any previous 'financial associations'. A financial association arises when someone takes out credit with another person, such as being jointly responsible for a mortgage.

Getting protected

People getting married may wish to take out one or more financial products to ensure financial stability should something unpleasant happen to either of them or their property.

Wedding insurance

For an outlay of about £50 to £100, they will have the peace of mind should the unthinkable happen: for example, the church burns down or the reception venue goes out of business.

The rings

Get those rings insured. Personal possessions cover generally provides better value than any insurance offered by a jeweller, because they are protecting all the possessions they regularly carry, not just their rings.

Gifts

Some contents insurance providers automatically increase cover by 10% for a month before and after a wedding. Others offer unlimited cover as standard. They need to establish where they stand.

Looking to the future

As it is obviously desirable that their partner is adequately provided for, should the worst happen, they should seriously consider taking out life insurance and possibly also critical illness cover and income protection. They should also write (new) wills and, if finances permit, ensure adequate pension funding for retirement.

Buying a property together

Getting married is a life-changing step that often goes hand in hand with buying a property. With the commitment of marriage comes a promise of permanency, so thinking about where to live becomes a consideration involving decisions about such things as the appropriate environment in which to bring up children, as well as long-term financial planning.

There are literally thousands of different mortgage products available on the market. Each type has potential advantages – and disadvantages, depending upon a couple's particular circumstances and the current and future state of the economy. People should equip themselves with as much financial knowledge as possible and should always seek *independent* specialist advice before choosing a mortgage provider.

The deed is done

Solicitors should ask house purchasers how they want the deeds to be worded. This question merits serious consideration by both parties when purchasing a property jointly as man and wife.

Property in England and Wales may be owned in an individual's *sole name* (for example, that of the husband or wife), or as *joint tenants*, or as *tenants in common*. Different rules apply in Scotland and elsewhere.

If two people own a property as joint tenants, then, when one of them dies, the other person will automatically become owner of the whole property (regardless of the terms of the deceased owner's will). If, on the other hand, two people own their home as tenants in common, each person only owns a share in the home (usually quantified according to their contributions to the purchase price). When one tenant in common dies, his or her share will pass into their estate and be dealt with by the personal representatives, under the terms of his or her will. Therefore a tenant in common can leave their share of the property to whoever they want, unlike a joint tenant.

Most married couples opt for the joint tenancy option. However, if your daughter already has children from a previous relationship and wishes to leave at least some of her property assets to them, or if she has paid more than 50% of the cost of the property, she would be wise to seriously consider the tenants in common option.

A final financial fact

Marriage is good for you! According to Andrew Oswald, Professor of Economics at Warwick University, getting married results in improved health, with a married person having a 9% lower risk of dying over a seven-year period compared with an unmarried one. There are also financial benefits to tying the knot, with married people earning between 10% and 20% more than their single colleagues. Equally importantly, according to the good professor, marriage brings the same amount of happiness as an income of £70,000 a year.

7 The Big Day

'I'm letting you go, but I'll never be far.
You can always reach me, wherever you are.' (Pearl Simmons)

Well this is it, Dad!

On the wedding day there are a number of traditional duties which you may be expected to fulfil. Be aware that there may be some variations to these according to the structure of your family and the wishes of your daughter. Maybe she wants both her father and stepfather to walk her down the aisle, or perhaps she wants her mother to do it. Whatever her choices, try to understand her reasoning and motives – and respect and accept her decisions.

Your responsibilities may also be affected, to some degree at least, by the religious or secular nature of the ceremony. Civil ceremonies in stately homes, other prestigious buildings, hotels and restaurants can often be more flexible than religious ones. This gives your daughter some scope to make a few variations to the service. However, they too still have certain rules and regulations which must be followed.

After the ceremony comes the reception. Whether you are the official host or technically a guest, your daughter is likely to appreciate your help and support during the festivities. While people will appreciate well-presented food, drink and entertainment, the biggest factor in any reception's success is the welfare and enjoyment of the guests.

Pre-wedding tasks

Early in the morning, all the mundane, everyday activities of normal life cease and everything is geared to the time of the ceremony. The bride, her mother and her bridesmaids will probably be virtually unapproachable and all the ordinary things that need to be done, phone calls to be made, dog to be walked, fall to you either to do yourself or to make sure someone else does them. In short, you become a sort of project manager but without the authority to change anything you feel isn't right.

Once the hairdressers, beauticians, dressmakers and other advisers have come and gone, the bride stands ready to dazzle all around her. Your main focus at this stage should be to help her approach her wedding with joy rather than stress. You also need to recognise and respond to the emotional turmoil her mum will be experiencing. But before you can do these things, you first need to understand what *you* are feeling – and why you are feeling it.

Acknowledging how you feel

Men are generally not brought up or encouraged to express their feelings – even to themselves. It is perfectly natural to be a little sad. Don't bottle things up. Acknowledge that this is a momentous day in your life too. You won't be able to support your daughter effectively until you have got to grips with your own emotions.

There's always a moment during the wedding day when it hits you. The gravitas may impact as you walk down the aisle, as you leave the church, as you dance with your daughter. Whenever and wherever it may happen, be totally assured that it *will* happen.

Throughout the day both of you will walk that delicate line between past and future. During this bittersweet transitional period your emotions will include everything from anxiety to hope, guilt to pride, fear to relief. You will be experiencing all the inevitable and often contradictory physical and emotional processes of letting go. And letting go is never easy.

The important thing is to understand that what you're feeling is normal, and that you are not the only father who has moments when he wishes he could turn back the clock and perhaps do one or two things differently.

Supporting your daughter

This is probably the most important day in your daughter's life, so far. Is it really surprising that she's a little nervous? Some last minute concerns will be logistical: 'What if there is a problem with the food?' Others will be psychological. The same girl who may have been so laid back over the last few months suddenly no longer wants to be the centre of all this attention. Yet the nervousness experienced by most brides-to-be stems from the realisation that life can never be quite the same again.

You should be able to reassure her that everything has been thoroughly planned and you have contingency plans in place should anything go awry. Remind her that it is perfectly natural to feel this way. She needs to recognise that nerves are simply the body's way of preparing for something special.

This is a time to be upbeat and positive. It is her Big Day. Everyone is on her side. She is about to begin an exciting new chapter of her life alongside the man she loves. Tell her she's not losing a father, she's gaining a husband.

Supporting her mother

With all the attention focused on your daughter, it is all too easy to forget what a massive day this is for her mother too. Like you, she is certain to be experiencing a crazy cocktail of often contradictory emotions. Along with the pleasure she is hopefully feeling, there's bound to be a lot of spoken and unspoken nostalgia in the air. After all, this is the day that begins the transition from her little girl to someone's wife.

This rite of passage can be an incredibly difficult time for mother and daughter alike. It's a push and pull that quite probably will not end until well into your daughter's first year of marriage. It's only at that stage that she will begin to feel comfortable enough with her new status that she no longer needs to continually remind everyone that she really is an independent, married woman.

And if the wedding involves divorced and/or remarried parents, relatives who at best tolerate each other, and perhaps even a son-in-law she does not even like, the stress levels can be off the scale.

If all this isn't enough for her to have to handle, how must she be thinking now you and your daughter will be in the spotlight as she's pushed to one side? She may well have been involved in all the wedding planning, but now tradition decrees that *you* accompany your daughter to the church, *you* walk her down the aisle, *you* hand her over to her new husband, *you* make that emotional speech and *you* dance with her at the reception.

Of course, you *should* have been discussing all these emotional and logistical issues with her mum for months, if not for years. Whether you have or not, you certainly need to now.

Talking and being affectionate

She is probably as nervous and uptight as your daughter, maybe more so. What if the car doesn't turn up? What if the chef is unwell? What if Uncle Steve drinks too much? What if . . . ? What if . . . ? What if . . . ? Reassure her that everything will be fine. Tell her what a fantastic job she has done, not only over the last few months, but over your daughter's entire lifetime – and mean it.

Whatever you do, don't allow either of you to lose sight of the romance that surrounds the day. Assuming the two of you are still together, remind her of *your* wedding day. Talk, hold hands, dance. Pay her a genuine compliment: 'You shouldn't look so beautiful; it isn't fair on the bride'.

Getting her to the church (almost) on time

After confirming that the cars have arrived as arranged to take the bridesmaids, mother of the bride and other members of the family to the ceremony, help your daughter into her wedding car (or whatever mode of transport is being utilised), making sure her dress is not crushed.

This maybe the only time you'll spend alone with your daughter all day, so make the most of it. Try to respond to her emotional state. She may wish to talk or may simply hold your hand in silence. If she's happy, that's wonderful. If she's nervous or sad, once again reassure her that things will be fine. Crack a joke or two to lighten the mood, so long as it doesn't annoy her. Even if she seems to be totally irrational, never argue or lose your temper. This is a day for unconditional support.

Bear in mind she's likely to be very nervous, so any words of comfort or wisdom you can offer will be appreciated. Have a few tissues handy too. She might need some – and so might you. As you arrive at the wedding site, seize the moment and say something simple, sincere and significant: 'You'll remember this moment for the rest of your life.'

Ceremonial duties

While your daughter, of course, is the star of the show, for the next few minutes you will also be taking centre stage. Try to relax and enjoy the moment – and encourage her to do the same.

Walking up the aisle

Traditionally, you stand with your daughter at the back and enter when the music begins. You are then followed by your daughter's entourage. Nowadays, however, many brides reverse the order of entry, following the American pattern. Perhaps flower girls enter first, followed by bridesmaids and ushers. Only once everyone else is seated, do you and your daughter make your dramatic entrance.

If your daughter prefers this variation, she needs to choose the right music. It could seem somewhat bizarre for two three-year-old girls to enter to the accompaniment of *Here Come the Bride*.

Stand to your daughter's right, arm in arm. As you walk down the aisle – or escort her into the register office or into any of the legally 'approved premises' – smile and nod to guests but concentrate mainly upon your daughter. This is another golden opportunity to say something heartfelt and memorable: 'Love one another and you will be happy. It's as simple and as difficult as that.'

Giving her away

If the marriage is taking place in a church, a hymn is usually sung once you have walked your daughter down the aisle. The vicar then states the reason for the gathering and asks if anyone knows of any reason why the marriage should not take place.

Having received the couple's agreement to be married, the vicar asks who is giving the bride away. The bride hands her bouquet to the chief bridesmaid and you place your daughter's right hand in that of the vicar, who gives it to the groom. The symbolism of this moment is clear and poignant. Your little girl is becoming a woman and you are passing responsibility for her to another. So don't just turn her in the general direction of the groom and scamper off to your seat. Make eye contact with both of them, smile, shake his hand firmly, give him a word of encouragement – and kiss your daughter. *Now* you can sit.

'I do'

Once vows and rings have been exchanged, the bride and groom lead the way to sign the register. They then walk back down the aisle, followed by the chief bridesmaid with the best man; any other attendants; the bride's mother with groom's father; and the groom's mother with you at her right-hand side.

The party then poses for the wedding pictures. Be guided here by the professional photographer who will know how to get the best results. Then everyone moves on to the reception. Traditionally, you accompany the groom's mother, usually in the third car – following the bridesmaids and best man. If there are only two official cars, you may decide to use your own vehicle, with your daughter's mum and the groom's parents as passengers.

Reception responsibilities

Whether it's a drinks and dinner do, an evening event, an afternoon-only affair, an evening buffet, or some other arrangement, you'll have some important duties to perform. As always, be prepared to be flexible, given your family circumstances and your daughter's wishes.

However formal the occasion, please don't spend so much time fretting about your obligations that you forget to enjoy yourself. Remember, without you, there may not have been such a wonderful wedding – or, come to think of it, even a bride. Take time out to relax, chat to people and accept compliments.

Get the ushers involved to give you more 'quality time' with your immediate family. And keep things in perspective. Perfection is of no consequence; logistical mishaps are trivial and unimportant. If anything does go a little awry, it will probably go down as a humorous and treasured family memory.

Greeting the guests

Traditionally there is a receiving line to greet the guests as they arrive at the reception or as they enter the room for the wedding breakfast. The bride's mother is first in line, followed by you and then *possibly* by other members of the wedding party. Etiquette is open to interpretation on that one.

The disadvantage of this procedure, especially at a big wedding, is that it can take an age to make small talk with every single guest. The newlyweds may prefer to welcome the guests on their own, or alongside the toastmaster or catering manager, leaving you to mingle, circulate, smile and make introductions.

An alternative arrangement would be for the bride and groom to make a triumphal entry *after* all the guests have arrived. As they arrive, they are greeted with a chorus of clapping, cheering, whistling and camera flashes.

Being the host with the most

Don't confine your attentions to the big groups of people who are obviously already having a good time. Take a good look around the room and see whether anybody is struggling to get a conversation going, or standing shyly on the sidelines. Go over and take the pressure off them by initiating a discussion, introducing timid types to other people or suggesting they check out the entertainment on offer.

Keep a close eye out for any youngsters who may be drinking too much and any elderly guests who may be flagging. Don't allow the wedding breakfast to become a dog's dinner. If a problem arises, remind yourself that it will *not* be a turning point in Western civilisation. Quietly sort it out without interrupting anybody else's fun. The golden rule of reception hosting is: Never panic!

Let me entertain you

You all need to think carefully about *what sort* of entertainment will be provided. It is not necessary to fill every minute but one or two fun activities during the reception are sure to go down well. It really is a case of less is more. You also need to consider *when* you'll want to provide a little fun and games. Perhaps it is during the 'quiet' period between dinner and dancing.

Activities that require concentration for long periods of time, like board games or quizzes, are best confined to smaller gatherings, while the all-pervading noise of karaoke all afternoon or evening will grate on people's nerves, especially if the person holding the microphone can't sing. That said, there may be a case for a little bellowing towards the end of the proceedings.

Physical activities are often the best way of breaking the ice between people who aren't great at small talk. If you've got the space – and the budget – try something everybody can have a go at, such as having a little flutter at a mini casino. Companies bring everything they need with them, from chips and croupiers to fun money and dice. Other options include caricaturists, silhouette artists and magicians.

Mood music

Atmosphere is important. You need to start on the right note. Whether it's recorded or live, background music helps sets just the right mood and gets guests ready to celebrate. 'Background' is the key word here. Your guests will be chatting, so keep the volume down.

Drinks

It is always a nice touch to offer your guests a welcome drink as they arrive. While a glass of bubbly is the traditional wedding beverage, remember that people may prefer something non-alcoholic, to start with at least. It's not necessary to wait on them hand and foot. Pour their *first* drink. Let everyone know where they can find refills. You really don't need to circle the room checking guests have a full glass.

Don't forget the children

Younger children in particular will soon become bored and potentially disruptive if they are expected to sit though a series of speeches and a seemingly endless number of photo opportunities. If you plan a few activities especially for them, *everyone's* day will be much more enjoyable – and peaceful. Here are some possibilities:

- Hire a professional nursery nurse

- Book a children's entertainer

- Arrange a treasure hunt

- Provide goody bags

- Provide a craft area where they can have fun and get creative

- Ask them to draw pictures of the wedding

- Show them a kiddies' DVD

- Give them a quiet place where they can 'de-hype'.

Surprise, surprise?

You may decide to give the happy couple – and the guests in general – a little surprise at the reception. Here's an idea to ponder. During the canapés, hand out balloons with postcards on the bottom and ask everyone to write a personal note on the stamped addressed card. Invite everyone outside and release the balloons.

For the next few months the newlyweds should be receiving cards from all over the country and possibly from overseas. To make it more competitive (and to encourage people to return the cards), you could offer some wine to the guest whose card travelled the farthest and some euros to the person who returned it. What's great about this surprise is that it keeps the memory of the wedding alive for weeks, during a time which can sometimes seem a little flat.

'Unaccustomed as I am . . .'

Some couples decide to have the speeches *before* the meal. This allows nervous speakers to get their speeches 'out of the way' so they can relax and enjoy the occasion. Most toastmasters and other wedding advisors counsel against this as tight catering schedules can be severely disrupted if speeches go on for longer than intended. Also, if there is no obvious highlight at the end of the meal, things can tend to fizzle out as individuals and groups of people migrate to the bar and elsewhere.

For these reasons, it is traditional for the speeches to take place *after* people have eaten. It is important to know who is going to speak, and in what order. Usually, the bride's father speaks first, especially if he is hosting the event.

Dancing the night away

Assuming that you are physically fit to do so, there is an expectation that the father of the bride will be involved in at least some of the dances. If you are really keen, you could go to lessons or buy an instructional DVD. Then again, you may decide to just shuffle around the floor, smiling and chatting. After all, it's not *Strictly Come Dancing* so you're not going to be slated by Craig Revel Horwood and the gang.

Being involved in the first dance

The first dance is usually announced by the band or DJ and it is taken as the official start of an evening reception. The groom escorts his bride onto the floor, after a chorus or two they are joined by the rest of the immediate wedding party. It is traditional for you to dance with the groom's mother. After a few more bars, you are joined by the rest of the guests.

Sharing the father-daughter dance

Whether you and your daughter are as graceful as Fred and Ginger – or as ungainly as Fred and Wilma – this can be a genuinely touching moment as you take the floor together for the second dance. And if you've secretly worked out a dance routine together, this can bring the house down.

It is important for you both to choose the right song. It should be meaningful to each of you, but the lyrics should also be appropriate to the occasion. While your selection should be personal, look for something memorable, inspiring; something that will melt the heart of daughter, father – and every onlooker. Here are just a dozen possibilities, any of which would be sure to go down well:

- My Little Girl (Tim McGraw)
- I Loved Her First (Heartland)
- In My Daughter's Eyes (Martina McBride)
- Butterfly Kisses (Bob Carlisle)
- Through the Years (Kenny Rogers)
- To Dance with My Father Again (Luther Vandross)
- Sunshine Sunset (Topol, Miriam Karlin and Company; *Fiddler on the Roof*)

- Lullabye (Goodnight My Angel) (Billy Joel)

- My Girl (The Temptations)

- Father and Daughter (Paul Simon)

- The Way You Look Tonight (Frank Sinatra)

- Unforgettable (Nat and Natalie Cole).

If some of these songs are new to you, it is well worth checking them out on YouTube.

Into the groove

At this stage the volume and tempo will be revved up to bring guests to their feet. Almost everyone will get up to dance at a wedding, especially after consuming a glass or two. While the actual playlist must be a personal choice, here is a selection of some classy and some cheesy dance songs which would be certain to get the party swinging. They span over 50 years and are listed in the order they were released (or, in some cases, some might argue, they escaped):

- Rock Around the Clock (Bill Haley and His Comets)

- Twist and Shout (The Beatles)

- Oops Upside Your Head (The Gap Band)

- Do the Conga (Black Lace)

- Locomotion (Kylie Minogue)

- The Only Way is Up (Yazz and the Plastic Population)

- Cotton Eye Joe (Rednex)

- Macarena (Los del Rio)

- Dance the Night Away (The Mavericks)

- We Like to Party (Vengaboys)

- Reach (S Club 7)

- Poker Face (Lady Gaga).

Encourage your daughter to choose a wide range of music that will include something for everyone. That means playing something by the Monkees as well as the Arctic Monkeys; something by Van Morrison as well as James Morrison.

The grand finale

Traditionally, the bride and groom would have left the reception shortly before the final dance. However, this does not always happen nowadays with newlyweds partying on until the celebration ends.

Aim to end proceedings on a high rather than allowing things to peter out. When you sense the moment is right, consult with your daughter and her new husband and then announce that final dance.

These days everyone tends to participate, singing and possibly linking arms or forming a circle around the newlyweds. This makes for a great climax as the happy couple are given a memorable send-off. Some favourites for this 'big finish' are:

- All You Need is Love (The Beatles)

- You'll Never Walk Alone (Gerry and the Pacemakers)

- Angels (Robbie Williams)

- Hi Ho Silver Lining (Jeff Beck)

- Auld Lang Syne (Traditional)

- Congratulations (Cliff Richard)

- Glad All Over (Dave Clark Five)

- I've Had The Time of My Life (Bill Medley & Jennifer Warnes)

- New York, New York (Frank Sinatra)

- That's Amore (Dean Martin)

- Viva Las Vegas (Elvis Presley)

- Walking On Sunshine (Katrina & the Waves).

Post-reception reflection

The cake has been eaten, the last glass of champagne has been drunk and the final guest has left. In a moment of silent reflection you will understand that from the moment your daughter spoke those small, massive words 'I do', your life could never be quite the same again. But a *different* life does not necessarily mean a *worse* life. If you act wisely and judiciously, this can be the beginning of an even stronger relationship between the two of you.

A girl always needs her father

Of course, you will always be her dad. A girl's dad can never be replaced and will always remain in her heart. She has simply begun a new chapter in her life. And so have you. As you let her go, you can be certain that she *will* come back to you. It's like holding quicksilver in your hand: leave your fingers open and it stays; clutch it and it darts away.

That gap-toothed little girl has become a woman. By encouraging independence within her marriage, you'll be opening up a doorway to an even richer, deeper understanding of each other – and a lifelong relationship to match.

Back to the future

Perhaps watching the two of them together reminds you so much of her mother and you at their ages, when your love was new and tender. Where did the years go? Why, it wasn't so long ago that *you* were the young lovers, then the young parents, working together to make a life.

Switch your attention from your daughter to her mother, who will need your reassurance, comfort and support. She too is facing a new situation without her daughter. Whether you are still a couple, or whether by now you have gone your separate ways, today is a happy day – a day to look to the future, but also to reminisce, a day to reflect upon precious family memories that will remain with the both of you forever.

Part Three

Making a Memorable Speech

8 Preparing Your Speech

'To create a memorable speech requires excitement, empathy, warmth, enthusiasm . . . and flair. Flair is the sizzle in the sausage.' (Bob Monkhouse)

Think of your speech as a gourmet meal. Your opening lines should serve up a tasty starter that really whets the audience's appetite for the main course. Your closing lines should provide a delectable and memorable dessert with a delicious aftertaste.

Your aim is to create an awe-inspiring and entertaining speech that will be remembered for years to come, and for the right reasons. Too much to ask? Well, no it isn't, if you follow the advice, tips and guidelines that follow.

Getting the tone right

Great speeches come from the heart. Every father is different; every father and daughter relationship is different; every extended family dynamic is different. Precisely what you say, and how you say it will be affected by these and other factors. However, regardless of your personal circumstances and the degree of formality of the wedding, it is undeniably true that this is an extremely important day in your daughter's life and your speech should reflect this. It should be:

Emotional

Don't stifle emotion. You should feel free to display strong personal feelings. Describe an incident or two that demonstrates the joy you and your wife have had bringing up your daughter and the pleasure you have found in getting to know your new son-in-law – and his family. However, you must be genuine. False heartiness, cheap sincerity and – worst of all – crocodile tears will be all too obvious to an audience.

Optimistic

This is not the time to share your personal woes, paint a gloomy picture of the present or offer dire predictions about the future. Stress your certainty that in her husband's care, your daughter will prosper along with him and – with a little homily on the 'give and take' necessary to a successful marriage – the confidence you have that happiness must accompany the love they so evidently bear for one another.

A tribute to the happy couple

Refer to some positive characteristics of both the bride and groom that are *well known* to the audience (perhaps speak of your 'devoted daughter' and her 'hard-working husband'). Then declare your confidence that they will make all the effort needed and will not be found wanting. This is a marriage made in heaven. They were made for each other.

Saying it your way

Don't buy a speech. It cannot be original, personal and relevant, no matter what 'personalisation' sites might tell you. If you accept the role, you shouldn't treat your speech as a chore where you look for an easy way out.

Many people have donated their speeches to wedding websites. Highly laudable, I'm sure, but they are of little value to a thinking father of the bride. If you crib jokes and one-liners from five-star speeches, the odds are that many in the crowd will have heard them spoken by other speakers who have cherry-picked exactly the same material. This will immediately undermine your entire speech.

What possible value can there be in relating someone else's sentimental reminiscence in your speech? None. Everything you say needs to be thoughtful and unique, a loving reminder that our imperfections are part of our charm, and the sentiments of love, family and friendship shared together on this day are the truly important wedding accessories.

Conveying emotion

What can make your speech gripping is its potential to *involve* the audience on a subjective level, to make them empathise with your deepest feelings, to forge a bond between them and you.

It's all well and good *saying* how much you care for your daughter, how confident you are that she has made the perfect choice of husband and how sure you are that they will have a wonderful future life together. The audience may well think, 'How nice', but they won't be moved.

Far too many fathers make the mistake of dwelling on their own feelings and reactions and can be stunned to discover that no one else in the room can relate to their genuine sentiments. 'But I was almost in tears as I was saying this', they protest. 'How could the guests not be similarly moved?' How indeed?

Emotions are abstract concepts

The problem is that our feelings are *abstract*. It is not that we do not hear or understand abstractions, but without a visual peg, without something we can conjure in our minds with colour and form, intangible ideas and concepts make little impact and are soon forgotten.

Two other factors are involved here, and neither has anything to do with the hardheartedness of the guests. Firstly, when we try to describe the physical symptoms associated with a particular emotion – be it sadness, happiness or delight – there is little room for surprise, for creating a wow factor. We all know how it feels first hand.

The paradox is that in order to hold an audience's attention, we need to provide some new or profound angle, spin or insight into these emotions. Yet how can we say something different and meaningful about universal feelings?

Secondly, no matter how original your description of your emotions, it does not alter the fact that that those emotions belong to *you*, not to *your audience.*

Talk about the incident, not the emotion

So what is the solution? The best way to convey your feelings is to focus upon an incident which illustrates them. Concentrate, not upon the emotion that was evoked, but on the situation which gave rise to it. Turn abstract ideas into strong, concrete mental images. What you must do is to take each guest by the hand and guide them through your valley of emotions without ever having to mention any of those emotions by name.

Don't bore the audience with long introductions or unnecessary explanation. Get straight to the heart of the matter. Focus on a single incident or situation; provide a snapshot and it will keep the image alive in their mind and heart. The more apparently mundane and ordinary the circumstances surrounding the occasion, the more powerful and extraordinary will be the emotion it evokes.

> *I keep all my important certificates and awards in a drawer in the living room – my 1975 BSc, my 1981 accountancy qualification, my 2009 Salesman of the Year award. But shall I tell you which certificate I treasure most? Compared to this one all the others pale into insignificance. I won it back in 1989; well actually I won it jointly. You can keep the BSc, the ACA and the Salesman of the Year . . . my most treasured award is the one for first place in the 1989 [daughter's school] Father and Daughter Egg and Spoon Race. That award means more to me than a Nobel Prize or an Oscar. We were a real team that day. And, [daughter], I want you to know that you'll always be in first place in my heart.*

People want more than to simply listen to stories, however well they may be told. They also want to experience one or two good, soul-satisfying lingering emotions. Think about your favourite books, music, films. Don't they all share this lingering quality? Your aim is to create a mental image that packs a real emotional punch, to use words and images that elicit just the right response.

Less really is more

As father of the bride, you are expected to indulge in a little emotional outpouring as you say how much you care for your daughter, declare your confidence that she has made the right choice of husband and include a few positive thoughts about love and marriage in general. The problem is that an unremitting, relentless stream of gushing, florid language can come across as pretentious and insincere.

The simple, yet highly effective solution to this apparent dilemma is to use sincerity and emotion with caution and restraint, to spread them thinly throughout your speech, like caviar, not pile them on thickly, like marmalade.

> *Memories allow us to smell roses in December.*

> *I am her father, but she is my hero.*

One or two well-chosen genuine expressions of your strong personal feelings will be far more effective and memorable than a whole series of half-hearted passing references to the pleasure and delight you are experiencing on this most happy of days.

Choosing the right stories

This is a day charged with emotional intensity. Be passionate. Passion is contagious.

You need to open your heart and display your feelings through the stories you relate. Ask yourself: Do I really want the guests to know every last detail of my daughter's Saturday morning tap-dancing lessons, or do I want to share something deeply meaningful and joyous in our otherwise crazy world? Well, which would you prefer to hear?

As the writer C.S. Forrester reminds us, 'There is no denying the fact that words spoken from the full heart carry more weight than all the artifices of rhetoric'. It has been said that life is made up of moments, may be a dozen or so times when something happens that literally changes your life. Can you recall a moment that revealed something significant about your daughter's personality or maybe one that had a profound effect on your relationship with her?

The great thing about a story is that you dream it as you tell it, hoping that others might be drawn along with you, and in this way memory and imagination and language combine to create spirits in the mind. The challenge is always to find that one story or anecdote that will illustrate precisely what you want to illustrate.

> [Daughter] had climbed a tree but couldn't get down. I said, 'Jump. I'll catch you.' 'What if you don't catch me?' she replied. 'I'll catch you. You must trust me.' Our eyes met and in a split second, both our different fears became one. 'Even I get scared at times', I said. 'Scared of what?' 'Right now', I said, 'I'm terrified that you won't trust me.' She smiled and, without any further hesitation, jumped, landing safely in my outstretched arms. She looked up at me and with unspoken words, we both said, 'We don't need to be afraid anymore. We trust each other.' It was a momentous moment in our lives.

Real life stories are unbeatable. Choose the right story and the whole room will get goosebumps.

Saying it with humour

However, people can only take so much emotion. The way to avoid guests overdosing on it is to enliven your sentimental reminiscences with gentle touches of humour. Everyone loves a good gag. If you can find a *relevant* joke, you are onto a winner. It will relax the audience and you. Matching your choice of material to the nature of the guests is easy when the group all know each other. At wedding receptions this is often *not* the case, so you must choose your jokes with care.

Let's assume that only half the crowd know the best man, Dave recently had a nasty bout of food poisoning while on his holidays. There is no need to bore the other half by bringing it up again in great detail. One simple gag will do the job:

> *It's fantastic to see Dave here today, fighting fit after his recent little problem. He went to Greece last month . . . had the shish kebabs all week.*

Now *everyone* present should find that amusing – with the possible exception of Dave.

Choose your material with ingenuity and reconsider it with care. Does the humorous line arise naturally from the serious words that precede it? Does its punchline act as punctuation at the end of a paragraph so that you can embark smoothly on the next topic?

Look into the mirror

Any speaker who cannot laugh at himself leaves the job to others. Poke a little fun at yourself before you poke fun at anyone else.

> *What a panic yesterday evening. I heard [daughter] say to her mother, 'Mum, I've still got so much to do and I want everything to be perfect. I'm determined not to overlook even the most insignificant detail.' And her mother replied, 'Don't worry, love, I'll make sure your father is there.'*

Your daughter

Don't forget that's it's her Big Day. And a few crass words can shatter it. Target any humour with extreme caution and care. Does she have a good sense of humour? If she's game for a laugh, then she's fair game.

> *[Daughter] had their joint credit card stolen last month. [Son-in-law] hasn't reported it as missing because the thief is taking less out each week than she was.*

Your son-in-law

Once again, don't be too cruel and consider how he – and his family – is likely to react to a little gentle ribbing.

> *In many ways [son-in-law] has become like a son to me. He doesn't take any notice of what I say, he's always answering back and he is threatening to eat us out of house and home.*

Your wife

Target a mild potshot in this direction only if you are sure it will be received by your good lady in the humorous spirit that you no doubt intended.

> *Being a romantic sort of girl, [wife] insisted on getting married in her grandmother's dress. She looked absolutely fabulous – but her poor old granny nearly froze to death.*

Be positively insulting

Funnily enough, a teasing jibe and a sincere compliment often fit well together, each reinforcing the other in a kind of verbal synergy. The trick is to first set up a situation which you can exploit with a teasing remark, before turning this into a genuine compliment.

When she was 16, [daughter] joined the string section of the town orchestra. She practised at home day and night. For years she was always harping on about something or other (pause). Well, angels do, don't they?

So try to sugar your jokes with praise.

Offering some words of wisdom

Rather than simply regurgitating the same old, clichéd pearl or trinket of wisdom that has been heard by a million other couples, try to personalise any advice you may wish to offer. Give the bride and groom (and everyone else in the room) the benefit of any relevant life lesson you have learned through success or failure. How can they apply this to *their* lives?

Last year, for our Pearl Anniversary, some old friends gave us a DVD copy of the original cine recording of our wedding. We were thrilled. They told us we'd have to be able to lip read to know what was going on because there was no sound. But that didn't matter at all because we remember the day like it was yesterday. My father-in-law, the late [his name], a true Yorkshireman, made a lovely speech and told us to always remember that money comes first and last. You've got to make it first, and then make it last. That advice has served us well for over 30 years and I now pass on his wise words, with immense thanks, to the next generation.

Adding a sparkle to your speech

There are a number of ways you can make your speech special and spellbinding. No-one is expecting you to be a great raconteur. However, there are a few tricks of the trade that can help give any speech a lyrical, almost magical quality.

Using words to be said, not read

Most people know how to write something intended to be *read*, far fewer know how to write something intended to be *said*. Indeed, many are unaware there is even a difference. We are used to writing things to be read. Such everyday written communication is known as *text*. What we are not so used to doing is speaking our written words out loud. Writing intended to be spoken and heard is known as *script*.

Every effective speaker must recognise that there are very important differences between text and script, namely:

Text	**Script**
– is a journey at the reader's pace	– is a journey at the speaker's pace
– can be re-read, if necessary	– is heard once, and only once
– can be read in any order	– is heard in the order it is spoken.

Therefore, you must prepare and present a speech for an audience which *cannot* listen at its own pace; which *cannot* ask you to repeat parts it did not hear or understand; and which *cannot* choose the order in which to consider your words.

We seem subconsciously to understand the best words and phrases when we *speak*, but we seem to loose the knack when we *write* script. Consider how the same sentiment might be conveyed by a writer, first using text and then script:

Text

> *The meaning of marriage is not to be found in church services or in romantic novels or films. We have no right to expect a happy ending. The meaning of marriage is to be found in all the effort that is required to make a marriage succeed. You need to get to know your partner and thereby get to know yourself.*

Script

> *The meaning of marriage isn't to be found in wedding bells . . . it isn't the stuff of Mills and Boon romances . . . there is no happy ever after, No, the meaning of marriage is in the trying and it's about learning about someone else . . . and through that learning about yourself.*

The lesson is clear: speak your words out loud before you commit them to paper. You will find that each element, each phrase, each sentence will build from what has gone before. Instinctively, you will take your listeners from the *known* to the *unknown*; from the *general* to the *specific*; from the *present* to the *future*.

As a speechmaker, you must:

- think like a listener, and

- write like a talker.

Using warm words

Words are powerful. They conjure images, evoke emotions and trigger responses deep within us so we react, often without knowing why. So-called *warm* words make us feel secure and comfortable, while *cold* words leave us uneasy and unsure. Writer Henry James said the two most beautiful words in the English language are *summer afternoon*, because they evoke just the right emotions.

> ***Love*** *fills your life with* **happiness***, gives you* **strength** *and* **grows** *beyond you. You feel* **warmed** *by their presence even if they're away. Distance cannot separate you. Near or far, you* **know** *they are* **yours** *and you can wait for them.* **Successful** *relationship* **grows** *between two people who really* **like** *as well as* **love** *each other.*

Painting word pictures

Today people spend more time *watching* TV and films than *listening* to the radio. They are used to visual images so you must give your speech a graphic quality by not telling the story, but by painting word pictures that allow your audience's imagination to take over.

> *[Daughter] and I loved going to gran's on a Saturday. Tea was lovely, fish and chips that gran didn't fetch from the shop but cooked herself, cream meringues and chocolate éclairs, tinned peaches with evaporated milk, the lot washed down with fizzy lemonade.*

Can't you just feel that gassy pop getting up your nose?

Using figurative language

Try to make your speech colourful and original. Similes and metaphors are particularly useful devices. A *simile* is a figure of speech, usually introduced by *like* or *as*, that *compares* one thing to another.

> *She was simmering **like** a corked volcano.*

A *metaphor* does not so much compare as *transform* one thing to another.

> *Marriage. Ever since humans gathered together in caves, they – we – have displayed a basic instinct for becoming couples. Your man and your woman. Your Romeo and your Juliet. Your yin and your yang. It's as natural as his and hers bath towels. If the life of humankind were music, they would all be duets. It's been a bit of a musical day one way and another. Violins in harmony with cellos. [Daughter] in harmony with [son-in-law]. The past in harmony with the future. And, as the Bard of Avon put it: 'If music be the food of love, play on'.*

Remembering rhythm

A good speech should attract and hold listeners as a magnet attracts and holds iron filings. Here are three simple techniques that can turn your words into music in an audience's ear.

The rule of three

Three is a magic number. People love to hear speakers talk to the beat of three. The effect of three words, three phrases or three sentences is powerful and memorable.

> *We wish you fun and excitement for today . . . hopes and dreams for tomorrow . . . and love and happiness forever.*

Parallel sentences

This takes the rule of three one stage further by beginning each sentence with the identical words. Sentences that are parallel add a rhythmic beauty and help an audience anticipate and follow your thoughts.

> *Marriage is a celebration of love. Marriage is a celebration of joy. Marriage is a celebration of life.*

Alliteration

The recurrence of sounds and syllables, usually at the beginning of words, can help create just the right mood.

> *Water your garden with **friendship, faith** and **favour**. And then watch it grow. You deserve a garden of love.*

93

Weaving in a couple of quotations

Everyone enjoys hearing a particularly witty or wise turn of phrase or apt quotation. However, very few quotes will be received with knee-slapping belly laughter or will cause a lump in the throat. Their merit usually lies in their encapsulation of a truth, a smart observation or a humorous example. Use them in moderation and keep them relevant to the personal circumstances and background of the couple.

> *I am reminded of a verse from HMS Pinafore: 'When he was a lad he served his term. As an office boy to an Attorney's firm. He cleaned the windows and he swept the floor. And he polished the handle of the big front door. He polished up that handle so carefullee. That now he's the Ruler of the Queen's Navee' – well, almost, anyway.*

Beginning and ending in style

People remember best what they hear first and what they hear last. Think of your opening and closing words as the verbal bookends of your speech. They must be strong enough to hold and support everything that comes between them.

Hooking the audience

Successful speechmakers often ponder, consciously and unconsciously for days over their opening words. They know that the first few sentences of their speech set the course for success or failure: a good start sets you plain sailing, a poor one makes you sail against the wind.

> *Ladies and Gentlemen, 'We cannot fully enjoy life until someone we love enjoys it with us.' Not my words, I'm afraid, but how I agree with them . . .*

Adding a topical reference

In the early part of your speech, it's a good idea to throw in a line or two about something funny, amusing or poignant that has happened earlier in the day. Your guests will know this reference could not have been planned and this ploy will help give the whole speech a feeling of spontaneity.

> *And what about that magnificent young cellist? She has attracted so much favourable comment that I simply have to give her a special mention.*

Ending on a high

Try to end with a flourish. Your concluding remark should be what the high note is to an aria: the candescence that triggers applause. If you can wrap up your speech perfectly, you will inject that ultimate bit of magic.

> *Marriage is a constant journey of understanding, fun, sorrow, forgiveness, laughter, sharing. In short, it is a journey of life, a journey of love. May your journey be a long one filled with joy.*

Making that toast

All you need to do now is add a few words after your big finish.

> *Ladies and Gentlemen, please stand, raise your glasses and drink a toast with me to the health and happiness of [son-in-law and daughter].*

> *To [son-in-law and daughter]!*

If you have two children, be careful not to marry the wrong one off, or marry them to one another. Let's say your children are Jane and Barbara and Barbara is getting married. You'll be used to putting their names together and it would be all too easy to fall into the trap of saying, 'Please raise your glasses to Jane and Barbara!' rather than, '. . . to Steve and Barbara!' Your family may think this is quite a laugh, but Steve's may not be quite so sure.

Bracketing your speech

This is a device usually associated with seasoned pros. It is designed not only to grab an audience's attention at the *start* of a speech, but also – and at the same time – set-up a situation that can be exploited at the *end*.

The idea of bracketing is to present your speech as a satisfying whole, not merely a series of thoughts, reminiscences and humorous asides. Here is an example of a possible pair of brackets. The words used at the end will include some which were planted clearly at the start.

Set-up

On such a day like this I hope I can be forgiven for indulging in a little daydreaming – both reminiscing about the past and predicting the future. Today we celebrate a marriage, the union of my daughter [daughter] and her new husband [son-in-law] . . .

Pay off

Now all this daydreaming must stop. It is time to move on. At the end of all my reminiscing, I've come to these inescapable conclusions: [wife] and I have done a lot for [daughter] . . . but she has done even more for us. Of course, she will always be our dear daughter, but there is no doubt in our minds that the time is now right to entrust her to [son-in-law's] loving care. And knowing [son-in-law] as we do, we are certain it will be very, very good care . . . (followed by the toast)

Notice how the repetition of the words *daydreaming* and *reminiscing*, together with the repetition of your daughter's and son-in-law's names help the open-and-closed nature of the brackets and provide a pleasing and memorable symmetry.

Keeping it flowing

Have you noticed how entertainers, politicians and news readers move easily and unobtrusively from one topic to another? Like them, you can keep your speech flowing naturally by making use of a few of these simple devices.

Bridges

A bridge is a word that alerts an audience that you are changing direction or moving to a new thought.

> *And she took the job in London.* **Meanwhile** *other developments were taking place . . .*

Triggers

A trigger is a repetition of the same word or phrase to link one topic with another.

> *That's what [daughter]* **was like** *at school. Now I'll tell you what she* **was like** *at college . . .*

Rhetorical questions

These are questions which do not require an answer. As well as serving as a way of keeping things flowing, they also allow you to pass on information to people without insulting the intelligence of those already in the know.

What can I tell you about a girl who won the school prize for chemistry, represented the county at netball and passed her driving test – at the sixth attempt?

Flashbacks

A sudden shift to the past is a far more interesting way of linking topics than simply listing events chronologically.

Today she is the confident woman-about-town you see before you.
But five years ago *she wasn't like that . . .*

Identifiers

An identifier is a word or phrase that keeps cropping up throughout a speech to help create an impression of a coherent whole, not merely a series of thoughts, observations and reminiscences. It also reinforces the audience's group identity.

*Look at **our** (not **the**) beautiful bride . . .*

We *(not **I**) wish them well . . .*

Pauses

This is a non-verbal way of showing your audience that you have finished one section of your speech and are about to move on to another.

Physical movements

If you turn to your daughter, the guests will know you are going to talk to her, or about her.

Quotations, jokes or stories

Any of these can also serve as an excellent link. Here a man-on-the-bus gag links a personal compliment about your daughter's good manners with a more general observation that everyone has played their part in making this a day to remember.

> *[Daughter] always shows good old-fashioned courtesy to her fellow human beings. A rare attribute today, I'm sure you'll agree. When she was on the bus last week she stood up to give an elderly gentleman her seat. He was so surprised, he fainted. When he came up he said, 'Thank you', and [daughter] fainted. Well I'm delighted to say there has been absolutely no shortage of courtesy here today. You've all been great. Things could not have gone better . . .*

Preparing your script

The best talkers are those who are most natural. They are easy, fluent, friendly and amusing. No script for them. How could there be? They are talking only to us and basing what they say on our reactions as they go along. For most of us, however, this sort of performance is an aspiration rather than a description. Our tongues are not so honeyed and our words are less winged. We need a script.

But what sort of script? Cards? Notes? Speech written out in full? There is no right way of doing it. Here is a simple method favoured by many speakers:

- Write the speech out **in full**

- **Memorise** the opening and closing lines and **familiarise** yourself with the rest of the speech

- **Summarise** the speech on one card, or one sheet of paper using **key words** to remind you or your sequence of stories, reminiscences and so forth.

The great advantage of this technique is that you won't forget huge chunks of your speech and you will come across as a natural and spontaneous speaker because you will be using your own words and phrases, not simply reciting a prepared speech.

The ideal approach, then, is to appear extemporaneous, to present a speech that is a happy compromise between one that is read word for word or learnt by heart, and one that is completely impromptu and unprepared. The key is to prepare the substance of what you will say, but not the precise words you will use to convey it. As actors are taught: 'Dig deep to fly high and then throw it all away.'

Putting it all together

Traditionally, as father of the bride you would have been expected to have included the following broad sections and messages in your speech:

- Hook your audience, introduce yourself and officially welcome guests on behalf of your family

- Give a special mention of any close friends or family who were unable to attend

- Thank everyone involved in the organisation (and funding)

- Express your pride in your daughter

- Welcome your son-in-law into the family

- Welcome his family

- Reminisce about your daughter's pre-wedding years

- Pay a tribute to your wife

- Proffer some personalised advice to the couple

- Wish them success and happiness for the future

- Propose a toast to the bride and groom.

You may well decide to follow this time honoured format. However, with so many social and demographic changes over recent years, this traditional approach may seem inappropriate to you. For example, if your daughter and/or new son-in-law is re-marrying, this would have a strong influence on the tone and content of your address. Or perhaps you will be sharing the stage with your daughter's biological father or her stepfather. In Chapter 11, you'll find examples of speeches written to suit a variety of family circumstances. These should help you to get the tone and content of your speech spot on.

Many of the most memorable father of the bride speeches were written with a common theme in mind: perhaps how the bride has continually overcome hardships and struggles, or maybe by providing a nostalgic picture of how she has developed from a stroppy youth to sensible young woman. A great speech will always incorporate many different thoughts and emotions, but they will all be connected under one overarching theme.

In a fairly informal setting, you could thank everyone for coming and then simply propose a toast. However, your daughter may feel a little short changed by this minimalist approach. As it's her big day, it is better to at least:

- Thank everyone involved in the organisation (and funding)

- Speak proudly of your daughter and welcome her new husband into your family

- Thank everyone for coming

- Propose a toast to the bride and groom.

So while it is perfectly possible to say everything you want to in just a couple of minutes, you may decide to take this golden opportunity to make a longer, more thoughtful public tribute to your daughter (and wife). A warm speech, full of memories, light anecdotes and gentle humour is certain to make your guests feel connected and contented. The emotion and humour you convey can be enhanced by showing a short film or some early years photos of your daughter as you speak.

Start early

When planning your speech, the best advice is to start early. Your most original and useful ideas will tend to occur at the oddest of times, so always keep a notebook handy. Try to create an interior 'film' in the listeners' heads through the words you speak and the mental images you create. Then forget about your speech for a couple of days. Allow it to simmer so you can return to it with a fresh perspective.

When you re-visit it, read it out loud. Immediately you will be aware of the parts that are spot on, the parts that need a little tweaking, and the parts that are simply not worth including. Once you're happy with each of the various sections of your speech, try to link them together naturally so the whole thing flows gracefully from beginning to end.

Let's now prepare a first draft of a father of the bride's speech, following the traditional structure. As we shall see in Chapter 11, you may well decide to change the order a little, combine or omit one or more sections, or perhaps add something entirely new. It all depends upon the background and circumstances of the bride, groom and their families.

The important thing is to make your speech unique, personal and relevant. In the same way as no woman wants to go to a wedding with the same dress as anyone else, a father of the bride should pride himself by not going to a wedding with the same speech as anyone else.

Hook your audience, introduce yourself and officially welcome guests on behalf of your family

'Love is a great force in life, it is indeed the greatest of all things.' So said E.M. Forster, and E.M. knew what he was talking about.

Ladies and Gentlemen, this is a truly historic day! This day, the 28th of June, will always be remembered for three world famous events, Henry VIII was born back in 1491, the British Lions roared to an amazing series win against South Africa in 1997, and on this day in 201X, [son-in-law] married [daughter]!

For those of you who don't know me, I'm [your name], and I'm [daughter's] dad. I'd like to start by welcoming, on behalf of [wife, daughter and son-in-law], the guests from both our families. It's wonderful to be surrounded by so many friends and family who have been so important to us during our lives. By your presence here today, you show friendship and love, and bring even greater joy to us all. Happiness and joy ring in the air.

A special word of welcome must go to Hans and Gretel, our dear friends who have flown in all the way from Holland to be with us today. It's amazing what some people will do for a free meal. Hans, I've got a couple of bottles of schnapps in. Thank you both so much for coming – dank U wel.

Well I don't know what the weather is like back in old Amsterdam, but it can't be any nicer than this. We have been so lucky that the sun has shone down upon us throughout this very special day. It's been an incredibly bright start for what is sure to be an incredibly bright future for you both, as man and wife.

Give a special mention of any close friends or family who were unable to attend

Unfortunately, Ian and Mary couldn't be with us today because Ian is unwell. I'm sure we all wish him a speedy and full recovery. I spoke to him yesterday and he told me to pass on their very best wishes and to say they would be raising a glass or two to you both this evening.

Sadly, as many of you will know, Uncle Robert passed away earlier this year. Although we all miss Bob terribly, we can all rejoice in the fact that he would have been absolutely delighted that [son-in-law] and [daughter] have now tied the knot. In a sense I feel he is celebrating here with us today because, like me, Bob knew you two were made for each other.

Thank everyone involved in the organisation (and funding)

Now weddings don't just happen. They take a fantastic amount of work and organisation. As most of you will already be aware, today's events were planned and co-ordinated with panache and precision by [daughter]. Without her things would not have run so smoothly or have been so fantastic and memorable. Over the last year she has displayed the patience of Job, the wisdom of Solomon and the organisational skills of, well [daughter]. I know I'm speaking on behalf of you all when I say thank you so very, very much. You couldn't have made a better job of it.

Express your pride in your daughter

You know, today really belongs to her – and, of course, to her co-star [son-in-law]. We are both so proud of [daughter]. She has the gift of finding joy everywhere and of leaving it behind when she goes. If she had a pound for every smile she's put on a face, she'd be a millionaire. And talk about being sensitive and caring. Last week she had to tell her class who'd been chosen for the school play – and who hadn't been. Those who hadn't been given a part were told they'd been given the vital job of sitting in the audience and clapping and cheering. Everyone was over the moon. That's what I call being diplomatic. Some of our politicians could learn a lesson or two from you. I'm so proud of you and I want the world to know it. You deserve such a perfect day as this.

Welcome your son-in-law into the family

And what about this debonair young man at her side? Well, quite simply, over the last few months we've come to the inescapable conclusion that he's exactly the type of person we'd always hoped [daughter] would marry: a man who knows where he's going in life and how he's going to get there. We're so impressed that he's such a hard-working, dependable and trustworthy man with absolutely immaculate tastes. After all, he supports United and he chose [daughter], didn't he? From the very first moment we saw them together, we knew they were the perfect match. Their devotion was obvious. Their affection radiant. Their love exploded like fireworks. [Son-in-law], we're so pleased to formally welcome you into the [your surname] clan.

Welcome his family

And an equally warm welcome goes to [son-in-law's] parents, [their first names]. We've all got to know each other really well over the last few months and I like to think we've grown into good friends. Of course, marriage is not only about finding the right person, it is about being the right person. What doubles our joy is the fact that, like us, you are certain that your son has found his perfect partner in life.

Reminisce about your daughter's pre-wedding years

Where were you on 28th June, 1983? In my case, I was at Anytown Hospital maternity ward. And, not surprisingly, so was [wife]. When a first child is born there are really three births – the birth of the child, the birth of the mother and the birth of the father. The entire world looked different to me from the moment she was born.

[Daughter] was always a very special daughter – kind, considerate, loving - and a source of great pride and joy as [wife] and I watched her grow. We shared her birth cries and smiled through her first steps, her first words, her first giggles. We beamed through school concerts, sports days and birthdays. We shared laughter and tears. Every passing year gave us events to remember and memories to cherish. As she grew, I recorded every special memory in my heart.

I remember one warm, quiet sunny afternoon when we were sitting hand in hand in the park. Not talking. Not doing anything really. A neighbour strolled by and said, 'So you're not busy today, [your name].' I smiled back politely, thinking to myself: I'm extremely busy, busy making memories.

When she was about ten she made her first little cake. It was a brilliant first effort. A few days later she made four individual cakes for the family only to find there were five of us home for tea that day. Immediately she announced that she never really cared for cakes herself. That's the kind of person she is. [Daughter] not only makes the best cakes, she makes the best memories too.

During her early teenage years, we had an old biscuit tin which we used to exchange letters and notes. 'Dad, I'm in the school play'; 'Dad, I got an A in Maths'; 'Dad, I love you.' It was wonderful. But imagine my horror the day I read that I was going to be a grandfather. What should I do? What should I say? That evening my unremitting panic turned to unmitigated relief when [daughter] told me her dog Suzy was going to have puppies.

When she went off to Uni, the tin got put away. Then, about a year ago, it mysteriously re-appeared. This time my message read: 'Dad, I'm getting married'. It was fantastic news. I wanted to shout for joy. In fact I did. I just hope it won't be too long before I get another little note saying I really am going to be a granddad.

Pay a tribute to your wife

The only trouble about being a grandfather, of course, is that you have to be married to a grandmother. Only joking, [wife]. But I really would like to take this opportunity to say I am the luckiest man in the world, not only to be blessed with such a wonderful daughter, but also to me married to the best wife and best mother in the world. It's not that she does any one thing that makes her the best wife in the world, it's all the little things she does for us. It's the understanding and the acceptance and the way she takes care of everything. It's the way she treats me, forgives me, puts up with me – and loves me. [Son-in-law], they say as a daughter gets older, she turns out to be more and more like her mother. If this happens to [daughter], you can ask for no more in life.

Proffer some personalised advice to the couple

Now it is customary on an occasion such as this for the father of the bride to pass on some words of wisdom about love and marriage. Well just before I got married back in 1980, my father gave us some invaluable advice which I now pass on to you two today. Dad produced a large sheet of white paper just like this one (hold up a sheet of paper) and drew a tiny black dot in the centre (do the same). 'What do you see?' he asked. 'A little spot', we replied. 'Anything else?' We looked hard at the paper and then at each other with blank expressions. 'You see a little black dot which represents the problems that you may face in the future. What you have both missed is all the white space that makes up the rest of the page. Good things can easily be ignored and taken for granted simply because they are so obvious. Always look beyond any tiny black spots and appreciate that huge white space.

Wish them success and happiness for the future

You are lucky people. Lucky to have found your best friend; lucky to be in love; lucky to know deep in your hearts that you're ready to share your lives together. A successful marriage involves falling in love many, many times – but each time with the same person. I am confident that you both have all the qualities needed to achieve this. Not only that, you both have the sense of humour, love and support for one another necessary to help you through any tiny black spots you may encounter – and the courage and determination to make sure white space is soon restored.

Propose a toast to the bride and groom

Ladies and Gentlemen, today has been blessed with spontaneity, the laughter of family and friends and – most importantly – the deep love between man and wife. Oh yes, and the excitement and joy of a very happy, very proud father.

There are only two lasting bequests parents can hope to give their children – one of these is roots and the other is wings. [Daughter], I believe over the years we have given you strong roots. Today, [wife] and I know the time is right for you to fly away from the nest with [son-in-law].

Ladies and Gentlemen – Friends, it is my pleasant and proud duty to propose a toast to the happy couple . . . to the love birds . . . to [son-in-law and daughter].

To [son-in-law and daughter]!

Rehearsing your speech

Why do some actors freeze or fumble on the opening night and then pick up a Lawrence Olivier Award six months later? It is the fear of unfamiliarity. As the days, weeks and months go by, the fear abates and the quality of performance improves.

Words become more familiar. Awkward juxtapositions are smoothed out. You suddenly think of a way of saying a stuffy sentence in a more straightforward and colloquial style. Some speakers like to rehearse, isolated and unheard, in a distant room, with or without a mirror. Others perform their speeches again and again to a sympathetic spouse or friend, either encouraging suggestions from them or requiring nothing more than a repeated hearing to ease away inhibitions.

Developing your comfort zone

Rehearse the beginning and ending of your speech to be spot on – and make sure you get the groom's name right. Rehearse the body of your speech not to be perfect, but to be *comfortable*. Audiences don't expect you to be perfect, but they *need* you to be comfortable. If you're not comfortable, they *cannot* be comfortable either. And if they are not comfortable, they *cannot* be fully receptive to your words of wit and wisdom, however hard they may try.

9 Delivering Your Speech

'This above all: To thine own self be true.' (William
Shakespeare; Polonius speaking in *Hamlet*)

Fortunately the guests understand what an emotional day this is for you. They are on your side and they are willing you to do well, so enjoy the limelight. Quite frankly, they won't give a damn if you fluff a line or two. All they want is to experience a genuine, sensitive, heartfelt speech. Every father wants to do his daughter proud and there can be no greater compliment than expressing his feelings in an eloquent and well-presented manner.

Finding your style

It is exceedingly difficult to discuss style and technique in general terms, since the ability to 'hold an audience', to be sober, sensible, yet amusing is such a personal business. However, there are certain 'rules' and guidelines which appear to be universal. Here they are.

Making the speech 'yours'

Did Elvis, Sinatra and Johnny Rotten all sound the same singing *My Way*? Of course not. The artist makes the crucial difference. So, too, does the speaker. Whatever individual characteristics you have that are special to you should be nurtured and cultivated and worked on, for it is those personal and unique quirks of appearance, personality and expression that will mark you out as a speaker with something different to offer. And that is never a bad thing.

Being passionate

What sets apart a speech that is remembered and one that has great content but is soon forgotten? It is the passion, purpose and personality that make the difference. You do not need to be an erudite, charismatic orator, but you do need to display genuine conviction, devotion and love.

If you have the burning desire to tell someone about something, you will have the enthusiasm necessary to do it and you'll find just the right words to express yourself. Tell the truth and speak from the heart. But the other side of speaking from the heart is listening to what your heart is calling you to say. The audience must believe that you believe. They will believe you only if you believe you.

Connecting with your audience

The writer E.M. Forster's mantra was: 'Only connect'. There is a huge difference between *impressing* an audience and *connecting* with them. The guests must be *certain* that you are sharing your innermost feelings – that you feel the truth of the subject, physically, emotionally, spiritually. They need to know you are breaking through clichés and moving into profound territory.

The ultimate connection is when you make each of them feel you are speaking *just to them*. In a vicarious way, they share *your* emotions, your memories, your experiences. At the same time, they silently contemplate *their* related emotions, their memories, their experiences.

The subject has become larger than itself. It has become a window into our world, an excuse for reflecting upon the most significant matters of the human experience. A bridge has been built; a bond forged. It is a wonderful feeling because an invisible chain now links every person in the room, regardless of age, gender, race, background or creed.

Being conversational

Sitting at leisure, with family, friends or colleagues, your conversation will be naturally relaxed and chatty, because that is the language of easy communication. When you make your speech, the words and phrases you use should be more considered, imaginative, creative and rhythmical than your everyday language, yet the way you say them, the way you deliver your speech should remain unaffectedly relaxed and chatty. Certainly you may need to speak a little louder or make other concessions to accommodate the needs of your audience, but, in essence, nothing in your delivery style should change.

Casual conversation is not structured in a literary way. You do not always finish your sentences. You repeat yourself. You use ungrammatical constructions – but you are obeying a different set of rules. You are obeying the rules of effective spoken communication which have been learnt, instinctively, down the ages. Don't abandon these rules when you speak in public. Talk to your audience just as you would to John and Jane Smith. What is the audience, after all, but a collection of John and Jane Smiths?

Being heard

You must be *audible*. If you are not, all else is lost. If there is a microphone available, get as much practice as you can and then use it. If there is no sound-enhancing equipment, speak as clearly and as loudly as is necessary to be heard. If the only other person in the room was at the back, you would talk to him or her naturally, at the right level, without shouting or strain, by:

- Keeping your head up

- Opening your mouth wider than usual

- Using clearer consonants

- Slowing down.

112

If you remember that you must be heard by that same person, at the back, during your speech, however many other people may be in the room, you will make those same four *natural* adjustments to your delivery.

Giving out the right non-verbal messages

We *speak* with our *vocal cords*, but we *communicate* with our *whole body*. An audience does a lot more than *listen* to a speech – it *experiences* it. Everything about a speaker's manner and demeanour contributes to the overall impression that the audience takes away.

So what hidden messages do you give out when you speak? If you are unsure, watch yourself in a mirror. Better still, get someone to record you. You may find that you need to work on one or more of the following. While each of these aspects of body language can be considered in isolation, a positive change made to any of them will also have a direct and immediate positive effect on the others.

Stance and posture

An aligned, upright posture conveys a message of confidence and integrity. Stand upright with your feet shoulder-width apart and very slightly turned out. You can then shift your weight from one side to the other, if you have to, without being noticed. Keep well clear of the table; leaning on it would make you look aggressive, and you could end up crying over spilt champagne. On the other hand, you may decide to walk about the room, moving among the guests as you give your address. If you take this approach, make sure you are near the right table when you talk to or about anyone directly.

Don't put your hands in your pockets or grasp them unnaturally at your back or front. Either hold any script or cue card in one hand or place it on the table in front of you. This allows you to glance at it from time to time while still giving you the freedom to use your hands to help express yourself.

Movement and gestures

Try to identify any potentially annoying movements or gestures which you display. The aim to eliminate them because such habits are a powerful means of distraction. Your audience will become preoccupied with them and will start *watching* you rather than *listening* to you and generally *experiencing* your speech.

Eye contact and facial expression

These are crucial aspects of effective communication because they gain and maintain an audience's attention and create rapport. Try to look around the room and from time to time focus on the guests farthest away. Include everyone as you speak. It is all too easy to end up having a private chat to the people closest to you.

But you must do more than simply look at your audience; you must use your eyes and your facial expression to help convey your *feelings*. This is not as difficult as it may sound. You do it every day. If you genuinely believe in what you are saying, your emotions will be revealed naturally through your eyes and your expression.

There is nothing more captivating than a smile. It shows a warmth and friendliness and says, 'I'm really pleased to be making this speech.' So smile, smile – and then smile again.

Once you begin to give out the positive silent messages about your feelings and emotions, you will become even more enthusiastic and eager – and this, in turn, will be reflected in your body language. You will have broken into a wonderful virtuous circle.

Thinking positively

Tell yourself you are going to make a great speech. And *believe* it. The largely untapped power of positive thinking really is immense. It has been estimated that 85% of performance is directly related to *attitude*. Unfortunately, many speakers think they are going to struggle, and this becomes a self-fulfilling prophesy. As Henry Ford put it: 'Whether you think you will succeed or whether you think you will fail, you will probably be right.'

Visualising success

Visualisation is the planting of mental images into the subconscious mind. These images have to be vivid and real – you must be able to *see*, to *hear*, to *smell*, to *touch*, to *taste* – and to truly *live them*.

When you can *imagine* an event over which you have some control happening, it will greatly increase the likelihood of it *actually* happening. This is not a crankish idea. Controlled medical experiments have proved it to be true.

You are now going to watch a film clip with a difference – because the screenwriter, the director, the cameraman and the star will be *you*. Close your eyes and visualise yourself rising to speak. You are looking good. Feel the warmth of the audience. You are surrounded by family and friends. You pause for a moment and then begin. They love your opening hook. But it gets better; your touching reminiscences and occasional jokes wow them. Laughter one moment, tears the next. They are eating out of your hand. Then comes that emotion-packed big finish, your verbal knock out. Nobody could have topped that. Listen to their cheers and applause. Now that's what I call a wedding speech!

Making fear your friend

Even the best-prepared and psyched-up speaker can suffer from a sudden attack of the collywobbles. It is perfectly natural and normal to feel a *little* nervous before delivering a speech. In fact, it helps if you do. The adrenalin will flow and you will be charged up and ready to give a really great performance.

However, if you feel *too* nervous, the quality of your speech will suffer. As you sit there, remind yourself that the audience is not a jury. They will readily forgive any little gaffs so long as you are genuine and sincere in everything you say.

Remember that 90% of nervousness is internal; only 10% displays itself to the outside world. You may feel shaky as you wait to be introduced, but the guests won't know that – unless you tell them. So *never* tell them.

Whatever you do, don't drink too much. Booze is like success; it is great until it goes to your head. As the late and great Bob Monkhouse used to say: 'Never accept a drink before you speak; never refuse one after.'

Meeting the guests

Try to talk to, or at least shake hands and exchange pleasantries with as many guests as possible before you speak, especially people you do not know. This will have a calming influence on you as subsequently you will not be talking to total strangers. Make one or two passing references to some of these people as you speak – but make sure you get their names right. If you do this, the whole of the groom's family and friends will feel far more included and your speech will come over as conversational, friendly and spontaneous.

Emergency relaxation techniques

If the pressure is really starting to get to you, try one or two of these pre-speech emergency relaxation techniques. They can be used anywhere and any time without anyone, except you, knowing it.

Stopping negative thoughts

1. Tell yourself: Stop!
2. Breathe in and hold your breath.
3. Exhale slowly, relaxing your shoulders and hands.
4. Pause. Breathe in slowly, relaxing your forehead and jaw.
5. Remain quiet and still for a few moments.

Sitting at a table

1. Pull in your stomach muscles tightly. Relax.
2. Clench your fists tightly. Relax.
3. Grasp the seat of your chair. Relax.
4. Press your elbows tightly into the sides of your body. Relax.
5. Push your feet into the floor. Relax.

Spot relaxation

1. Imagine your shoulders are very heavy.
2. Hunch them up.
3. Drop them down slowly.
4. Gently tip your head forward and feel the muscles pulling up through the middle of your shoulder blades.
5. Move your head gently backwards and feel the tension in the muscles down the front of your neck.
6. Bring your head back to an upright position and breathe in very deeply for a few moments.

Coping during your speech

Most people's nerves will evaporate once they are introduced and they begin to speak. Think about it this way: most footballers feel nervous, especially before a big game. But once they hear the shrill of the first whistle, their nerves seem to disappear. The reason? At that moment all their pent up tension is released and they can finally get on with the job in hand.

However, if you are still feeling a little jittery as you begin your address, these tips will help you cope:

- Smile naturally and find a few particularly friendly faces. Maintain plenty of eye contact with them. As your confidence grows, look more and more at other people around the rest of the room.

- Never admit that you are the slightest bit nervous.

- Keep your notes on the table so they can't be heard rattling, be seen shaking or end up all over the floor.

- Don't draw attention to your hands.

- Don't hold a hand-mike. Leave it on its stand.

- If your mouth feels dry and your throat tightens up, take a sip of water.

However, always remember that the greatest antidotes to nerves are preparation and attitude. If you prepare well and have a positive attitude, what used to be called fear can be re-named excitement and anticipation.

10 Great Speech Material

'A carefully chosen piece of poetry or prose can often express what we are feeling more eloquently than we could ourselves.' (Rev. John Wynburne)

Here is a collection of famous – and not so famous - quotations, poems, readings, blessings and toasts about love and marriage. They vary in tone and style – from classic to contemporary, from familiar to fresh – and can serve as a great source of inspiration when you are planning your speech. Choose no more than one or two that you feel are personal, memorable, wise, inspirational – and wholly appropriate.

Quotations

'Live so that when your children think of fairness, caring and integrity, they think of you.' (H. Jackson Brown, Jr)

'Occasionally in life there are those moments of unutterable fulfilment which cannot be completely explained by those symbols called words. Their meaning can only be articulated by the inaudible language of the heart.' (Martin Luther King, Jr)

'Treasure the simplest of things. The grand events will come, and you will feel pride, but when you need comfort and direction, you will find it in the simple things.' (Bernice Smith)

'There are only two lasting bequests we can hope to give our children. One of these is roots, the other wings.' (Hodding Carter)

'The most important thing a father can do for his children is to love their mother.' (Theodore Hesburgh)

'Marriage is that relation between man and woman in which the independence is equal, the dependence mutual, and the obligation reciprocal.' (Louis Kaufman Anspacher)

'Matrimony is a high sea for which no compass has yet been invented.' (Heinrich Heine)

'Marriage is not just spiritual communion and passionate embraces; marriage is also three meals a day and remembering to carry out the rubbish.' (Joyce Brothers)

'The greatest of all arts is the art of living together.' (William Lyon Phelps)

'Marriage resembles a pair of shears, so joined that they cannot be separated; often moving in opposite directions, yet always punishing anyone who comes between them.' (Sydney Smith)

'Love is the wine of existence.' (Henry Ward Breecher)

'Love is more than gold or great riches.' (John Lydgate)

'Love is the only weapon we need.' (Rev. H.R.L. Sheppard)

'To love is to place our happiness in the happiness of another.' (Gottfried Wilheim Leibniz)

'If your hearts are bound together with love; if both are yielding and true; if both cultivate the spirit of meekness, forbearance, and kindness, you will be blessed in your home and in the journey of life.' (Matthew Hale)

'It is a lovely thing to have a husband and wife developing together. That is what marriage really means; helping one another to reach the full status of being persons, responsible and autonomous beings who do not run away from life.' (Paul Tournier)

'Love is the light and sunshine of life. We cannot fully enjoy ourselves, or anything else, unless someone we love enjoys it with us.' (Sir John Avebury)

'The future belongs to those who believe in the beauty of their dreams.' (Eleanor Roosevelt)

'Marriage is three parts love and seven parts forgiveness.' (Langdon Mitchell)

'Love has the magic power to make a beggar a king.' (Emma Goldman)

'The most vital right is the right to love and be loved.' (Emma Goldman)

'Kindness is the life's blood, the elixir of marriage. Kindness makes the difference between passion and caring. Kindness is tenderness. Kindness is love, but perhaps greater than love . . . kindness is goodwill. Kindness says: I want you to be happy.' (Randolph Ray)

'Partnership, not dependence, is the real romance in marriage.' (Muriel Fox)

'No human relation gives one possession in another – every two souls are absolutely different. In friendship or in love, the two side by side raise hands together to find what one cannot reach alone.' (Kahlil Gibran)

'Chains do not hold a marriage together. It is threads, hundreds of tiny threads which sew people through the years. That is what makes a marriage last.' (Simone Signoret)

'Love understands love; it needs no talk.' (Frances Ridley Havergal)

'There is only one happiness in life: to love and be loved.' (George Sand)

'A marriage makes of two fractional lives a whole; it gives to two purposeless lives a work, and doubles the strength of each to perform it; it gives to two questioning natures a reason for living, and something to live for; it will give a new gladness to the sunshine, a new fragrance to the flowers, a new beauty to the earth, and a new mystery to life.' (Mark Twain)

'What greater thing is there for two human souls than to feel that they are joined together to strengthen each other in all labour, to minister to each other in all sorrow, to share with each other in all gladness, to be one with each other in the silent unspoken memories?' (George Elliot)

'Man and wife, a king and queen with one or two subjects, and a few square yards of territory of their own: this, really, is marriage. It is true freedom because it is true fulfillment, for man, woman and children.' (D.H. Lawrence)

'The sum which two married people owe to one another defies calculation. It is an infinite debt, which can only be discharged through all eternity.' (Goethe)

'There is nothing nobler or more admirable than when two people who see eye to eye keep house as man and wife, confounding their enemies and delighting their friends.' (Homer)

*'Immature love says: "I love you because I need you";
Mature love says: "I need you because I love you".'* (Confucius)

'Love is composed of a single soul inhabiting two bodies.'
(Aristotle)

*'Those who wish to sing always find a song.
At the touch of a lover, everyone becomes a poet.'* (Plato)

'Marriage is our last, best chance to grow up.' (Joseph Barth)

*'The goal in marriage is not to think alike, but to think
together.'* (Robert C. Dodds)

'Laughter is the shortest distance between two people.' (Victor
Borge)

*'Coming together is the beginning.
Keeping together is progress.
Working together is success.'* (Henry Ford)

*'There is no greater happiness for a man than approaching a
door at the end of a day knowing someone on the other side
of that door is waiting for the sound of his footsteps.'* (Ronald
Reagan)

*'In most good marriages, the woman is her husband's closest
friend and adviser.'* (Nancy Reagan)

'The first duty of love is to listen.' (Paul Tillich)

*'Being married is like having somebody permanently in your
corner, it feels limitless, not limited.'* (Gloria Steinem)

*'It takes two to make a marriage a success and only one a
failure.'* (Herbert Samuel)

'The secret to having a good marriage is to understand that marriage must be total, it must be permanent, and it must be equal.' (Frank Pittman)

'Happy marriages begin when we marry the ones we love, and they blossom when we love the ones we marry.' (Tom Mullen)

Anonymous but not forgotten

Many timeless wedding lines and verses have been passed down through the ages and generations until no one knows who first spoke or wrote them. Although none of the following words and sentiments can be attributed to anyone in particular, they are no less powerful and pertinent for that.

Every heart sings a song, incomplete, until another heart whispers back.

It has been written that when children find true love, parents find true joy.

The most important thing in life is to love someone. The second most important thing in life is to have someone loving you. The third most important thing is to have the first two happening at the same time.

Love doesn't sit there like a stone, it has to be made, like bread; re-made everyday, made new.

What makes a relationship work is having things in common. What makes a relationship passionate is having differences.

Happiness is to be found among life's common things. It is not great wealth, great learning, great genius or great power; it is not these things that make the possessors happy. It is health, friendship, love at home; it is the voices of children, it is sunshine. It is the blessings that are the commonest, not those that are the rarest.

The way to happiness? Keep your heart free from hate and your mind from worry. Live simply. Expect little. Give much.

Two things doth prolong thy life: A quiet heart and a loving wife.

To the world you might be one person, but to one person you might be the world.

The cure for love is marriage and the cure for marriage is love again.

A smile is the light in the window of your face that shows that your heart is home.

A Touch of Humour

Some people can be as wry as they are romantic – as witty as they are wise – and it is their ability to look at even the most important occasion with a tongue firmly planted in their cheek that offers brides' fathers the chance to incorporate some more light-hearted musings into their speeches. However, a word of warning: by all means include some gentle humour, but do so with extreme care. Don't shatter your daughter's big day by delivering a thoughtless line. To say: 'Marriage isn't a word, it's a sentence' is a great line for a stand-up comedian, but it has absolutely no place in a wedding speech.

'Now what is a marriage? Well my dictionary describes a wedding as the process of removing weeds from one's garden.' (Homer Simpson)

'Most girls seem to marry men who happen to be like their fathers. Maybe that's why so many mothers cry at weddings.' (Jenny Eclair)

'I haven't lost a daughter, I've gained an overdraft.' (Jack Dee)

'Some people ask the secret of a long marriage. We take time to go out to a restaurant two times a week. A little candlelight, dinner, soft music and dancing. She goes Tuesdays, I go Fridays.' (Henry Youngman)

'Every man needs a wife because things sometimes go wrong that you can't blame on the government.' (Dave Gorman)

'Marriage is a mutual partnership if both parties know when to be mute.' (Groucho Marx)

'Marriage halves our griefs, doubles our joys, and quadruples our expenses.' (Vincent Lean)

'Never go to bed mad. Stay up and fight.' (Phyllis Diller)

'As for my secret to staying married: my wife tells me that if I ever decide to leave, she is coming with me.' (Jon Bon Jovi)

'Only two things are necessary to keep one's wife happy. One is to let her think she is having her own way, the other, to let her have it.' (Lyndon B. Johnson)

'To keep your marriage brimming,
With love in the loving cup,
Whenever you're wrong admit it;
Whenever you're right shut up.' (Ogden Nash)

'Laugh and the world laughs with you, snore and you sleep alone.' (Anthony Burgess)

Poems, readings and blessings

To avoid possible issues of copyright, if you wish to reproduce a piece of writing (for example, in the Order of Service), it is best to choose one written by a person whose identity is unknown, or by a person who died over 70 years ago. To the best of my knowledge, all of the following contributions meet one or both of these criteria.

Poems

Destiny

Somewhere there waiteth in this world of ours
For one lone soul, another lonely soul,
Each chasing each through all the weary hours,
And meeting strangely at one sudden goal.
Then blend they, like green leaves with golden flowers,
Into one beautiful and perfect whole;
And life's long night is ended, and the way
Lies open onward to eternal day.
(Sir Edwin Arnold, 1832–1904)

When Two People Are at One

When two people are at one
in their inmost hearts
They shatter even the strength of iron or bronze.
And when two people understand each other
in their inmost hearts
Their words are sweet and strong,
like the fragrance of orchids.
(From the *I Ching* – Chinese; 12th century BC)

Boundless Goodwill

This is what should be done by the man and woman who are wise, who seek goodness, and who know the meaning of peace.

Let them be fervent, upright, and sincere, without conceit, easily contented and joyous, free of cares; let them not be submerged by the things of the world; let them not take upon themselves the burden of worldly goods; let their senses be controlled; let them be wise but not arrogant, and let them not desire great possessions even for their families. Let them do nothing that is mean or that the wise would reprove.
(From *Buddhist Scriptures*, 2nd – 3rd century AD)

Look to This Day
Look to this day.
For it is life,
The very life of life.
In its brief course lies all
The realities and verities of existence.
The bliss of growth,
The splendour of action,
The glory of power.
For yesterday is only a dream,
And tomorrow is only a vision
But today, well lived,
Makes every yesterday a dream of happiness,
And every tomorrow a vision of hope.
Look well, therefore, to this day.
(A Sanskrit Poem)

Welcome
When our daughter was a little girl,
We often used to say
How proud and happy we would be
On this, her Wedding Day.

Our daughter is not lost to us,
In fact, we've gained a son;
We're happy you have shared our joy
And seen them joined as one.

So may we welcome all of you
And may this whole day be
A happy and a joyous one
For friends and family.
(Author unknown)

On Your Wedding Day

Today is a day you will always remember,
The greatest in anyone's life.
You started off the day just two people in love
And ended it as Husband and Wife.

It's a brand new beginning, the start of a journey
With moments to cherish and treasure,
And although there'll be times when you both disagree,
These will surely be outweighed by pleasure.

You'll have heard many words of advice in the past,
When the secrets of marriage were spoken.
But you know that the answers lie hidden inside,
Where the bond of true love lies unbroken.
(Author unknown)

Love is Giving

Love is giving, not taking,
Mending, not breaking,
Trusting, believing,
Never deceiving,
Patiently bearing
And faithfully sharing
Each joy, every sorrow,
Today and tomorrow.
(Author unknown)

Marriage is a Promise

A marriage is a promise
That two hearts gladly make.
A promise to be tender,
To help, to give and take.

A marriage is a promise
To be kind and understanding,
To be thoughtful and considerate,
Fair and understanding.

A marriage is a promise
To share one life together . . .
A love-filled promise meant to be
Kept lovingly forever.
(Author unknown)

True Love

True love is a sacred flame
That burns eternally,
And none can dim its special glow
Or change its destiny
True love speaks in tender tones
And hears with gentle ear,
True love gives with open heart
And true love conquers fear.
True love makes no harsh demands
It neither rules nor binds,
And true love holds with gentle hands
The heart that it entwines.
(Author unknown)

Life's Lessons

After a while
You learn the difference
Between holding a hand
And chaining a soul.
You learn that love isn't leaning,
But lending support.
You begin to accept your defeats
With the grace of an adult,
Not the grief of a child.

You decide to build
Your roads on today,
For tomorrow's ground
Is too uncertain.
You help someone to plant a garden
Instead of waiting
For someone to bring you flowers.
You learn that you have been given
The strength to endure,
And that you really do have worth.
(Author unknown)

Quiet Thoughts

The quiet thoughts
of two people a long time in love
Touch lightly
Like birds nesting in each others warmth

You will know them by their laughter
But to each other
They speak mostly through their solitude.

If they find themselves apart
They may dream of sitting undisturbed
In each other's presence,
Of wrapping themselves warmly
In each other's ease.
(Author unknown)

Dove Poem

Two doves meeting in the sky
Two loves hand in hand eye to eye
Two parts of a loving whole
Two hearts and a single soul

Two stars shining big and bright
Two fires bringing warmth and light
Two songs played in perfect tune
Two flowers growing into bloom

Two Doves gliding in the air
Two loves free without a care
Two parts of a loving whole
Two hearts and a single soul.
(Author unknown)

Before we move on from poetry, why not consider writing a verse or two yourself? What better way is there in showing your daughter, son-in-law and everyone else in the room how you are feeling on this special day? You don't need to be a Wordsworth or a Tennyson to express your feelings. All that matters is that what you say is genuine, heartfelt – and perhaps humorous.

I am indebted to my stepson Stuart for these final three offerings:

A Father's Job

Well here we all are
On my girl's wedding day,
And I'm really hoping I can find the right words to say.
I could just pick some old lines from words said before,
But when it comes to my daughter,
She deserves so much more!

A father's job is never done,
With a daughter or with a son.
From the day they are born
Through their childhood days,
The cuts and the grazes
And all those school plays.

We watch as they grow,
As they cry and they laugh,
Always there when needed
To show the right path.
They fly the nest,
Too soon we may feel,
They are all grown up now:
Can this be real?

My job as father will never be done.
I wish you the best and welcome a son.
Your father's love will always be true;
I'll be here forever
For your groom and for you.

The Right Words

In so many of these speeches,
Made since time has begun,
Folk told not of losing a daughter,
But of gaining a son.

But clichéd words
Are not what I will use.
The medium of rhyme
Is what I will choose.

I tried so hard to find
All the right words to say
To the happy couple
On their most special day.

I will keep this short,
Which will please you, I think.
You are all waiting for the toast
So you can have a drink.

Now please charge your glasses
Because this rhyme's nearly done.
Let's drink to my daughter
And to my new son,

Let's wish them the best,
From all in the room.
Ladies and Gentlemen:
To the bride and the groom!

A Man of Few Words

A beautiful day and a beautiful bride;
This room full of people, me beaming with pride.
A man of few words, with so much to say,
My beautiful daughter on this, her wedding day.

I could tell you some jokes
Or tales of her as a child,
When she first held my hand
Or the times that she ran wild.

The good times and the bad,
So many silly fights,
Me so full of worry,
So many sleepless nights.

But we shouldn't look at yesterday
Or what has gone before;
I look at them so happy,
Who could ask for any more?

So here's to the future
And all that it may bring.
I'm a man of few words
But will say just one more thing:

On this beautiful day,
In this beautiful room,
Ladies and Gentlemen:
To the bride and the groom!

Readings

On Marriage

Then Almitra spoke again and said, And what of Marriage, master?
And he answered saying:
You were born together, and together you shall be forevermore.
You shall be together when white wings of death scatter your days.
Aye, you shall be together even in the silent memory of God.
But let there be spaces in your togetherness,
And let the winds of the heavens dance between you.

Love one another but make not a bond of love:
Let it rather be a moving sea between the shores of your souls.
Fill each other's cup but drink not from one cup.
Give one another of your bread but eat not from the same loaf.
Sing and dance together and be joyous, but let each one of you be alone,
Even as the strings of a lute are alone though they quiver with the same music.

Give your hearts, but not into each other's keeping.
For only the hand of Life can contain your hearts.
And stand together, yet not too near together:
For the pillars of the temple stand apart,
And the oak tree and the cypress grow not in each other's shadow.
(Kahlil Gibran, 1883–1931) (From *The Prophet*)

Bible (1 Corinthians 13:4-8a)

Love is patient and kind; love is not jealous or boastful; it is not arrogant or rude.

Love does not insist on its own way; it is not irritable or resentful; it does not rejoice at wrong, but rejoices in the right.

Love bears all things, believes all things, hopes all things, endures all things.

Love never ends.

The Meaning of Marriage

The meaning of marriage begins in the giving of words. We cannot join ourselves to one another without giving our word. And this must be an unconditional giving, for in joining ourselves to one another we join ourselves to the unknown.

The condition of marriage is worldly and its meaning communal, no one party to it can be solely in charge. What you alone think it ought to be, it is not going to be. Where you alone think you want it to go, it is not going to go. It is going where the two of you – and marriage, time, life, history, and the world – will take it. You do not know the road; you have committed your life to a way.
(Author unknown)

The Key to Love

The key to love is understanding . . .
The ability to comprehend not only the spoken word
But those unspoken gestures,
The little things that say so much by themselves.
The key to love is forgiveness . . .
To accept each others faults and pardon mistakes
Without forgetting, but with remembering
What you learn from them.
The key to love is sharing . . .
Facing your good fortune as well as the bad, together.
Both conquering problems, forever searching for ways
To intensify your happiness
The key to love is giving . . .
Without thought of return,
But with the hope of just a simple smile
And by giving in but never giving up.
The key to love is respect . . .
Realising that you are two separate people, with different ideas.
That you don't belong to each other,
You belong with each other, and share a mutual bond.
The key to love is inside us all . . .

It takes time and patience to unlock all the ingredients.

It is the continual learning process that demands a lot of work . . .

But the rewards are more than worth the effort . . .

And that is the key to love!

(Author unknown)

Blesssings

Native American Wedding Blessing

Now you will feel no rain, for each of you will be shelter to the other.

Now you will feel no cold, for each of you will be warmth to the other.

Now there is no loneliness.

You are two bodies but there is one life before you, and one home.

When evening falls you will look up and your love will be there.

You'll take their hand and they'll take yours and you'll turn together to look

At the road you've travelled to reach this – the hour of your happiness.

Apache Blessing

May the sun bring you new energy by day,

May the moon softly restore you by night,

May the rain wash away your worries

And the breeze blow new strength into your being,

And all of the days of your life may you walk

Gently through the world and know its beauty.

Irish Blessing

May God be with you and bless you;

May you see your children's children.

May you be poor in misfortune,

Rich in blessings,

May you know nothing but happiness

From this day forward.

Traditional Blessing

May this be the start of a happy new life

That's full of special moments to share.

May this be the first of your dreams come true

And of hope that will always be there.

May this be the start of a lifetime of Trust

And of caring that's just now begun.

May this be the day that you'll always remember,

The day when your hearts became one.

(Author unknown)

Toasts

It is customary for the father of the bride to round off his speech with a toast to the happy couple. You could choose one of the following that seems particularly apt, or you could combine two or more of them, or perhaps the elements of any that appeal to you, to create a perfectly personalised toast.

When children find true love, parents find true joy.

Here's to your joy and ours, from this day forward.

Here's to the groom with a bride so fair,
Here's to the bride with a groom so rare.

May their joys be as bright as the morning, and their sorrows but shadows that fade in the sunlight of love.

Here's a toast to love and laughter and happiness ever after.

Here's to her husband and here's to his wife,
May they be together for the rest of their life.

May you grow together like flowers and grass,
And may your life be a dance to the music of love.
May your joys be as bright as the morning,
And your sorrows but shadows that fade in the sunlight of love.

May this be the start of a happy new life that's full of special
moments to share.
May this be the first of your dreams come true and of hope that will
always be there.
May this be the start of a lifetime of trust and of caring that's just
now begun.
May today be a day you'll always remember; the day when two
hearts became one.

May we all live to be present at their golden wedding.

Down the hatch to a wonderful match.

Here's to the bride and here's to the groom,
And here's to the bride's father who paid for this room.

Much happiness to the newlyweds from the oldlyweds.

11 Sample Speeches

'The bride's father should be solid, thoughtful and sensible –
but he should also allow the lighter, more humorous side of his
personality to shine through.' (Gyles Brandreth)

A great wedding speech is always personal, genuine and one hundred percent heartfelt. The degree of emotion conveyed and the style and tone you adopt must be your decision based upon many unique factors and influences, including your personality, your daughter's personality and the relationship that exists between the two of you. If you feel uncomfortable saying something, don't say it.

While it's entirely up to you how you decide to play it, the important thing is that your speech should give the entire proceedings a human quality and dimension. Get it right and it will add a special touch to your daughter's day that money simply cannot buy.

Sample Speech 1

(Traditional and emotional, about ten minutes to deliver)

Ladies and Gentlemen, Boys and Girls, it is with total pleasure that I welcome you all to today's joyous event. For those of you who don't know me, I'm Roy, Claire's father – and my wife Joan and I are absolutely delighted that you were all able to join us here today on this momentous occasion. We feel truly honoured that you are here to share with us this most special of days.

Sadly though, two people who had a huge influence during Ben and Claire's formative years passed away earlier this year. Of course I am referring to Ben's

Uncle Joe, and my dear mother, Claire's Nanny Rose. In a sense, though, I feel they are both here in spirit, celebrating with us on this most glorious of days. Ladies and Gentlemen, I would like to offer the first toast of the day: Absent friends.

Now weddings don't just happen; they take a lot of preparation and hard work. So I would like to take this opportunity to thank everyone involved. In particular, I would like to express my sincere gratitude to Joan and her sisters Peg and Mavis who are sitting over there. Yes, that terrific trio really came up trumps. They have worked tirelessly over the last few months organising this reception. I know that an awful lot of time and effort has gone into the planning and I am sure you will all agree that it is a tremendous success and that they are all to be congratulated.

Well, what can I tell you about my gorgeous daughter, Claire? She is the ultimate people person. Her priorities in life are about as selfless as it gets: friends and family always come first; then it's her job, and only finally it's herself. And, believe me, anyone who can call her friend or family is truly fortunate. I remember her school's Sports Day back in 1990. Claire was a really good runner and was one of the favourites to win the girls' 100 metres sprint. She was right up there with the leaders when a girl next to her fell and twisted her ankle. Claire immediately stopped running, turned around and helped the injured girl up. She put the girl's arm over her shoulder and they slowly walked and hobbled the rest of the race together. As they both crossed the line all the spectators stood up and cheered wildly. It was a magical and memorable moment. Claire, I admire you as much as I love you. Today I am bursting with pride. You are the daughter every parent dreams of having.

And what about that dashing young man sitting alongside you? Ben, one of my abiding memories of today will always be the moment you slipped the ring on my daughter's finger. You know, from the time a daughter is born, every father anticipates this happening – some with joy, others with fear. Claire first brought Ben home to help us celebrate our Pearl Wedding Anniversary. It soon became very apparent that our other guests merely made a pleasant background for their love, and that for each of them there was but one other person in the room. Throughout the day we witnessed gentle looks, swift glances, silent gestures.

They were both full to the brim with delicate laughter, with childlike wonder, with tranquil love. We all took a part in their gracious happiness. It was clear they were meant for each other. Ben, since I first met you, I have been anticipating that moment you slipped on the ring with uncontrollable and unconditional joy. In you, I find the perfect match for my daughter.

Ben, you will find that our family is a circle of love and strength. With every birth and every union, the circle grows. Every joy shared adds more love. Every obstacle faced together makes the circle stronger. Ben, today Joan and I are delighted to formally welcome you with open arms into our family circle.

We are also honoured to welcome into our fold two other lovely people who haven't had a mention yet, but without whom Ben certainly wouldn't be here today. No, I don't mean those two charming people serving behind the bar. No, I mean Ben's parents, Alice and Denis, already our valued friends. Welcome to you both.

Now, in my youth, Claire's Nanny Rose used to tell us that every hand has its glove. As a child I wasn't too sure what she meant by that, but as I got older I realised what she was saying was that for everyone in this world there is someone else out there who is their perfect fit. The hard thing is to find that person. But once you have, everything else is simple. I know that's true because I had the miracle of finding my perfect fit with Joan. And I'd like to take this opportunity to thank you, Joan, for not only being a brilliant, tolerant wife, but – equally importantly – an outstanding mother and the guiding influence in the upbringing of our daughter, culminating in today's celebrations. You are my glove, my perfect fit. And when I see our daughter and her husband here today, I see that each of them, too, has found their perfect fit.

It is customary, at this stage, for the father of the bride to offer a few words of advice to his daughter and new son-in-law. Well, I've already told you a little about Claire's selfless priorities in life so perhaps my advice should reinforce this powerful theme.

To be honest, I didn't learn an awful lot at school. I spent most of my time avoiding work and really being a bit of a pain to my teachers. Looking back now, of course, I realise that was very silly. But I did learn one vital life lesson which has remained with me to this day and I will now pass on my teacher's wise words of wisdom to the two of you.

It seemed like just another average sort of day. I had no reason to think it was going to be anything but another boring lesson. How wrong I was. Our teacher stood in front of the class with a strange combination of items in front of him. He picked up a very large and empty jar and filled it with rocks, all about two inches wide. Then he asked us if the jar was full. We agreed that it was. He then picked up a box of pebbles and poured them into the jar and shook it lightly. The pebbles rolled into the open areas between the rocks. He then asked us again if the jar was full. We agreed it was. Next he picked up a box of sand and poured it into the jar. Of course, the sand filled up everywhere else. He asked us once more if the jar was full. We responded with a unanimous 'Yes'. He then produced two cans of beer from under the desk and poured the entire contents into the jar, effectively filling the empty space between the grains of sand. We all laughed out loud.

'Now', said our teacher as the laughter subsided, 'I want you to recognise that this jar represents your life. The rocks are the important things – your family, your children, your health, your friends – and if everything else was lost and only they remained, your life would still be full. The pebbles are the other things that matter like your job, your house and your holidays. The sand is everything else – the trivial stuff. If you put the sand into the jar first, there is no room for the rocks or pebbles. The same goes for life. If you spend all your time and energy on the trivial things you will never have room for the things that are really important to you.

At this stage curiosity got the better of me. I raised my hand and asked what the beer represented. Our wise old teacher smiled and said, 'I'm glad you asked. The beer just shows you that no matter how full your life may seem, there's always room for a couple of beers with a friend.'

Yes, that was the most important lesson I have ever had and I like to think it has served me well throughout my life. Pay attention to the things that are critical to your happiness. Spend time with your family. Take your partner out to dinner. Walk together under the stars. There will always be times later to clean the house and mow the lawn. Concentrate on the rocks of your life first – the things that really matter. Set your priorities. The rest is just sand.

Ladies and Gentlemen, please now stand and join me in a toast to the happy couple. Ben and Claire, you have both been fortunate in finding your perfect fit – in finding your rock. May your hands be forever clasped in friendship and your hearts forever joined in love. Ladies and Gentlemen: The bride and groom!

Sample Speech 2

(More modern and humorous, about ten minutes to deliver)

Ladies and Gentlemen, I'd like to thank you all for being here today, especially those of you who knew I'd be saying a few words, but decided to come anyway. I'm Dave, Sophie's dad, and I am absolutely delighted you could all be here with us today. Actually, this is the first time I've spoken at a wedding – except during other people's speeches.

Now a wedding is a fantastic opportunity for a big party, and today is no exception. We are delighted to have so many people here with us today: aunties, uncles, cousins, grandparents, friends . . . and a few people I actually recognise. You have travelled from all over the world: Tonga, Mongolia, Belize . . . are the only places *not* represented. It's amazing what some people will do for a free meal.

But before I get into my speech, I would like to pause for just a moment to remember two wonderful people who sadly can't be with us today: Sophie's grandmother – my mum Ruth – and Alan's grandfather George. Of course, some of you may also have friends and relatives who knew the happy couple, but are no longer with us. Wherever they all are today, I know they will be smiling down on Sophie and Alan with joy and with pride. And with that in mind I would like to propose the first toast of the afternoon. Please raise your glasses and drink to absent friends.

As most of you know, I'm in sales. I like selling things. I don't like giving things away. And today, I had to give away my daughter. I thought long and hard about this, and eventually I realised I had to give Sophie away or there could never have been a wedding. Why? Because before you sell anything, first you have to value it, to give it a price. And, believe me, no one could afford to pay the price that would be set by the value that I put on my daughter. She is priceless.

Well I'm sure you'll all agree that things could not have gone better today, so I'd like to take this opportunity to thank everyone who has been involved in all the planning and financing of today's fun and festivities. In particular, I'd like to thank Alan's parents, Pat and Bill on behalf of the bride and groom, for their help and generosity. It has been a real joint effort.

Like me, I am sure you two have a million memories of your child's wonderful growing up years. Sophie has been a brilliant daughter, and has provided my wife and me with 20 years of uninterrupted happiness. I know she's 25, but for the first five years of her life she was a right little nightmare. When she was a little girl she used to lift her dress over her head and pretend it was a veil. Fortunately, she's acquired a little more finesse since then. And how I remember that day she came home from school and told us that she'd been doing cartwheels all day because the boys had told her she was so good at them. I said, 'Sophie, they only want you to do cartwheels so they can see your knickers.' And she replied, 'I know that, Dad. That's why I took them off first.'

Now research tells us that women tend to choose husbands with characteristics farthest from those of their fathers. So I had very mixed emotions today when I heard my wife Linda describing Alan as handsome, hard-working and generous. However, it's true and it gives me enormous pleasure in formally welcoming him into our family. Welcome, Alan. I have no doubt about your qualities as a husband: you're honest, reliable and loving. But I reserve judgment about you as a son-in-law. Will you pop round to mine every weekend, or will I still have to clean the car and mow the lawn myself?

Today is a celebration, but not just of the love that has united Sophie and Alan in holy matrimony, but also of the families that have created, moulded and influenced the lives of these two special people. So Linda and I would also love to extend a very warm welcome to Pat and Bill and their family and friends. Thank you all for joining us in celebrating this special day.

Apparently it is now customary for me to say something about how wonderful my daughter is. Well, Sophie is simply the best. We are truly honoured and proud to call ourselves your parents. No parents could hope for a bitter daughter ... sorry, a better daughter. Sophie, your handwriting is atrocious. No, seriously, these really are my own words and feelings. I have so many magnificent memories of you.

When putting this little speech together, I was getting a bit sentimental so I decided to get out a few old photo albums. Tears welled up in my eyes as I turned those pages of mirth, magic and memories. One particular picture stood out from the rest. It was a striking image of our precious daughter lying on a rug, dribbling and pointing at the camera lens. What a treasure she looked as she tried to stand up on those wobbly legs. None of us will ever forget her 18th birthday party.

Oh yes, I have so many wonderful memories of Sophie in her childhood. Linda will probably recall that infamous day when Sophie was really playing up. Her mum told her to behave herself. 'I will for a fiver,' Sophie replied. And her mother said, 'Sophie, you should be good for nothing, just like your father.' Then there was the time I had a terrible throat. I couldn't eat, drink or even talk. When the doctor called, Sophie said to him: 'Dad's got a drinking problem. What can you do to help him?'

I'm delighted to say Linda and Sophie have always had a brilliant mother and daughter relationship and I would like to take this opportunity to publicly thank Linda for being such a fantastic mother and wonderful wife.

Now tradition demands that before I sit down I offer some profound words of wisdom that have been passed down from generation to generation and, no doubt, have been ignored by all of them. So here goes. Love is not just looking at each other and saying: 'You're wonderful.' There are times when we are far from wonderful. Just ask Linda about me. No, love is looking in the same direction. It's about linking our strength to pull a common weight. It's about pushing together towards the far horizons, hand in hand. It's about knowing that when our strength falters, we can borrow the strength of someone else who cares. It's knowing we are not alone in life.

Today you both said, 'I do.' Wonderful as that was, at the end of the day, these are mere words. You now need to back them up with actions. Happiness in marriage is not something that just happens. A good marriage has to be created. Always remember that in marriage the little things are the big things. It is never being too old to hold hands. It is remembering to say, 'I love you' at least once each day. It is never taking each other for granted; the romance shouldn't end with the honeymoon, it should continue through all the years. At times it won't be easy but, believe me, it will be so worth it when you look into your partner's eyes at your child's wedding – as I did today – and you say, 'I still do.'

Sophie and Alan, before I receive my standing ovation, I would like to offer a short toast:

Here's to the past – for all that it taught you,
Here's to the present – for all that you share,
And here's to the future – for all that you can look forward to together.

Ladies and Gentlemen, please raise your glasses.
The toast is: Sophie and Alan – bride and groom!

Sample Speech 3

(Short and sweet, about 2 minutes to deliver)

Good Ladies, afternoon and Gentlemen . . . I *knew* I should have rehearsed this speech. I'd just like to take a moment or two to thank everyone who has helped make this day so special. In particular, our gratitude must go to Dave's parents Sandra and Karl for sharing the cost of today's festivities, and to Dave and Kate for doing so much planning, organising – and spending!

I was so proud today to see Kate as she swept down the aisle. Proud and surprised – I'd never seen her sweep anything before. But seriously, no one could have asked more from a daughter. You deserve happiness and with Dave I am confident you have found it.

Dave is a very hard-working lad and we are all very proud of his recent success with his NVQs. When he asked me for Kate's hand, I asked, 'Dave, do you think you are earning enough to support a family?' 'Yes,' he replied. 'Think very carefully now,' I added, 'after all, you know there are six of us.' Only joking, Dave. But I do want you to know you really are one of the family now.

Looking around me, I see a picture of sartorial elegance. You'd put the Royal Ascot crowd to shame. But my wife isn't quite so sure about my appearance. As we were on our way to the wedding this morning, Nikki turned to me and said, 'You know, you don't seem quite as well dressed as when we got married 32 years ago.' 'Well I don't know why not,' I replied, 'because I'm wearing the same suit.'

But enough about my troubles. This day belongs to Kate and Dave and I think we should now drink a toast to them, don't you? Everyone who knows them is certain that this is a marriage made in heaven, and I know that you will all want to join me in wishing them a long and happy married life together. Ladies and Gentlemen, please stand and make sure your glasses are fully charged – mine is being charged to Mastercard. Please raise your glasses and drink to the health and happiness of Kate and Dave.

To Kate and Dave!

Sample Speech 4

(Second marriage, about seven minutes to deliver)

Reverend Jones, Ladies and Gentlemen – Friends: 'We cannot fully enjoy life unless someone we love enjoys it with us.' Not my words, I'm afraid, although how I agree with them. Good evening, everyone, I'm Steve, Jo's father, and it is an honour for me to be speaking to you on this wonderful occasion. I am delighted that so many of you were able to join us here. You are all very welcome.

Regrettably, however, others cannot be with us and, at this point, I would like to mention a few important people who have been so influential in Andy and Jo's lives. To begin with, my mother, Jo's Nana Vi. She is unable to attend due to her health needs. She has doted on Jo for 38 years. She may not be in this hall, but she is certainly in our hearts. Then there is my father Mark who passed away last summer. He would be so proud today. In a sense, I feel he is with us. No champagne for him though; he would have far preferred to be sipping his pint of bitter. And we mustn't forget Andy's parents Albert and Gwen who will both be looking down upon us from the stars. But they are all here in spirit, and they will all be celebrating with us on this their very special day. Ladies and Gentlemen, please remain seated as you join me in a toast to absent friends.

Now while all marriages are special occasions, a second marriage is an unsurpassable event because no one goes into it looking through rose-tinted glasses. This is a bright new start and, if you will forgive the cliché, today really is the first day of the rest of your lives. Jo and Andy, I know I speak for everyone in the room when I wish you a fantastic future together.

We are not losing Jo; we are merely entrusting her into Andy's care. And as we have got to know you, Andy, we have come to the inescapable conclusion that this will be very, very good care. You have shown yourself to be exactly the sort of person we had hoped Jo would marry: a dependable, hard-working man with a great sense of humour. Andy, it is an honour for my wife Jane and I to formally welcome you into our family.

Jo, you have always been a fantastic daughter and a magnificent mother to our granddaughter Chelsea. You know, you don't need a metal detector to find a real treasure. Jo, you are pure gold. When you were Chelsea's age – just three – we went to a wedding and I picked you up and danced with you in front of the band. At first you were so excited by the music, the lights, our dancing, but as we moved around the room, your head fell gently onto my shoulder and soon you were fast asleep. I held your tiny frame, so light, so delicate, so frail, and I vowed at that moment that I would always be there to protect you.

Today we will dance together once again, but – more importantly – you will be dancing with Andy. And Andy, I want you to promise me that you will make that very same vow during your dance – that from now on it will be you who will always be there to protect our precious daughter.

And that precious daughter wouldn't have grown into the loving, caring, giving individual you see before you today without the influence and impact of her mother. Jane, I don't tell you this as often as I should, but you have been a wonderful wife, a magnificent mother and great grandmother. No, that's ageing you a bit – a generous, glorious and gorgeous grandmother.

Tradition now demands that I pass on a few words of advice to the newlyweds. Well, today has been magic but it is important to realise that love is more than verses on valentine cards or lines from romantic films. Love is here and now, real and true, the most important thing in our lives. Love is the creator of our favourite memories and the foundation of our fondest dreams. Love is a promise that is always kept, a fortune that can never be spent and a light that never fades.

Whatever you may do, please never, never, never take your partner for granted. My dear mother Violet once told me about a long-married couple. Every night the husband ate a generous portion of casserole. Every night over the course of five decades, he consumed that same meal, wiped his face with a cloth, looked lovingly at his wife, smiled and spoke in a tender voice, 'That's the best meal you've ever cooked.' Now I'm not saying it will be casserole for you two every night, and I don't even know which of you will be doing the cooking. What I do know is that those simple words of appreciation sounded like sweet music to that elderly lady. Learn that lesson. Never take each other for granted.

You know, it has been said that marriage is like fine wine – not properly judged of till the second glass. This is the time for you to find true happiness. And it is an honour for us to be here to share this new beginning with you. We are certain that you will both receive all the joy you so richly deserve. Ladies and Gentlemen, please join me in a toast to the health and happiness of Andy and Jo.

To Andy and Jo!

Sample Speech 5

(Second marriage, about five minutes to deliver)

Ladies and Gentlemen, this is a truly historic day! This day, the 18th of November, will always be remembered because of three earth-shattering events. Appropriately named Richard Byrd became the first man to fly over the South Pole back in 1909, soccer's Ryan Giggs dribbled for the first time in 1973, and on this day in 201X, Angus married Emma!

For those of you who don't know me, I'm Dave, Emma's dad – and a very proud and happy dad, too. As father of the bride I have the privilege of making the first speech and paving the way for the star speakers, the groom and the best man. I think the ink is still wet on their speeches.

It is so gratifying that you were all able to join us here today to celebrate a marriage I believe to have been made in heaven. Each and every one of you has been so important to our family. And looking at you all today, I see before me the past, the present and the future.

Now someone once said that marriage is a lot like the army; everyone complains, but you'd be surprised at the large number that re-enlist. Angus, I'm delighted you have re-enlisted because, as I've got to know you over the last year or so, I've become aware of how much you two are in love. I have come to know that you are perfect for each other. To be honest, I cannot explain how or why I know this. But I do know it. Helen Keller put it far better than I ever could: 'The best and most beautiful things in the world cannot be seen or even touched. They must be felt with the heart.' Deep down within my heart I feel – indeed I know – the love between the two of you to be perfect, powerful and passionate. I see love pouring out of your eyes and it melts my heart.

Emma, you are a wonderful daughter. You know, children are a great comfort to you in your old age. Mind you, they sometimes help you reach it faster as well. Today you are a considerate, polite, well-mannered lady, and I am so proud of you. But you haven't always been like that, have you? I remember the day when you picked up your burger with both hands and crammed it into your mouth. 'Another bite like that, young lady' I told you, 'and you'll have to leave the table.' 'Another bite like that,' you replied, 'and I'll have finished it anyway.'

Tradition demands that I now offer you two a little advice as you pause at a crossroads with the past stretching behind you and the future lying ahead. Yes, an exciting journey is about to begin. Expect to face a long and winding road. At every turning be prepared for new discoveries, renewed hopes, plenty of laughter – and an occasional tear.

Well, if I have learnt anything from my time on this planet, it is to let your love always be stronger than your hate or anger. Learn to compromise; it is better to bend a little than to break. Believe the best in people rather than the worst. People have a way of living up, or down to your opinion of them. And remember that true friendship is the basis for any lasting relationship. The person you have just married deserves exactly the same courtesies and kindnesses that you show to all your other friends.

Life is for living. Mark Twain once said that when you look back on your life twenty years from today, you will probably be annoyed not at things you have done, but at things you have *not* done. Now, I'm not advising you to be a spendthrift, be foolish or take any unnecessary chances. Far from it. No, what I am saying is life is too short. Make the most of it. Enjoy yourselves. Follow your dreams.

Winding up, I would like to remind you that you are both very lucky people. Lucky to have found your best friends; lucky to be in love; lucky to know deep in your hearts that you're ready to share the rest of your lives together. Emma and Angus, make sure that you always remain friends, believe the best in one another – and follow those dreams.

Ladies and Gentlemen, the toast is: Emma and Angus; the bride and groom!

Sample Speech 6

(Divorced or separated natural father, about two minutes to deliver)

Good afternoon everyone. For those of you who don't know me, I'm Jim, Becky's father and I feel truly honoured to have been asked to say a few words on this her wedding day.

Of course, I am absolutely delighted that Becky has found her Mr Right in Leroy. During the time I've known you, Leroy, I like to think we've become good friends. Like Becky, you are a generous, warm-hearted individual and I am confident you will bring the best out in one another.

I have so many cherished memories of Becky I could share with you today. But the simple single memory I will treasure the most takes me back to her fifth birthday. It had been raining non-stop for over a fortnight but on her birthday, symbolically, it stopped. I remember seeing Becky rush into the middle of the garden where she spread her arms wide, raised her face to the sun and span round like a top. My heart soared, seeing my little girl, how she could celebrate life, how she could take such joy out of such a simple thing as a sunny moment on a warm September's day. That memory will stay with me forever.

Becks, it's fantastic that you've always looked towards the future with that same optimism and joy that I saw on your face that birthday afternoon. And I can see it again here right now. You're moving into your future with your arms wide open and your face turned to the light. Leroy, you've married a genius in the art of living and in the art of life. Learn from her – as I have – as you enter a wonderful new chapter in life.

Now Becky, of course, I can't take full credit for the wonderful person you have become. Although you've got my wicked sense of humour, you've undoubtedly inherited your brains and beauty from your mother. Pam, you have done a brilliant job in raising Lucy.

It now gives me great pleasure to propose a toast to the health and happiness of Becky and Leroy.

Ladies and Gentlemen, the bride and groom!

Sample Speech 7

(Stepfather, about five minutes to deliver)

Ladies and Gentlemen, we are told that marriage is a lottery. Well if it is, then these two people have hit the jackpot. They are both special people who were meant for each other. Hello, everyone. For those of you who don't know me, I'm Ray, Susie's stepdad and it is my privilege to make the first speech here this evening.

Firstly, on behalf of Susie and Matt, I would like to wish a very warm welcome to all the relatives and friends who are here today to celebrate their marriage. I know that some of you have travelled long distances to be here – from Scotland, Ireland, and London – and others a bit closer to home – from Bristol, Cardiff and Bath. Thank you all for coming to be with us on this very happy occasion. I hope that you are all having a wonderful day.

Although it brings a touch of sadness, I can't let this moment pass without mentioning three people who have meant so much to us but who sadly can't be here with us today. On Susie's side we remember her father's mum, Nanny Barbara and my dear dad, Jim. On Matt's side we remember his mum, Ellen. They are all sadly missed here today. However, I'm certain that they are here in spirit, and that they would be very proud today. So, ladies and gentleman, may I please ask you to remain seated, but to join me in raising your glasses as I make the first toast of the day: Absent Friends.

I'll be honest with you, it was a little tricky when I first married Sheila. Having never married before and with no children of my own, I wasn't sure what my role as 'father' was. I talked to lots of people who all gave me contradictory advice.

I read some books and blogs, which made me even more confused. I really had no idea what to be to Susie. Luckily, I didn't have to – she made the decision for me. Something wonderful happened. Without any encouragement from me or Sheila, one day Susie casually called me 'Dad'. Such a simple word, but one unfamiliar to me. It was wonderful and I thank you eternally for saying it.

From the very first day I came on the scene, Susie brightened up my life, and she has continued to do so ever since. Now when she was a small child we used to sit around and make up little rhymes about this and that. Do you remember? And while I'm certainly no poet, just for old times sake, I thought it would be a nice idea to compose and recite a little verse that will illuminate why my days of darkness – or my rather nights of darkness – disappeared once I had I met you:

Susie, my darling,
You made my life so bright.
I'll tell you the reason:
You never switched off the light.

Matt, you are so lucky to have met my little girl. Then again, she is lucky to have met you. You have shown yourself to be a reliable, hard-working young man. Matt, we are particularly proud and humbled by the way you selflessly took care of your late mother Ellen. Susie, you have just married a gem and, at this point, I would like to formally welcome your husband Matt into our family. I've decided I haven't lost a daughter I've gained a plumber. You're really handy around the house, and no call out fees. Welcome, Matt. I only wish I had a second stepdaughter. You never know when you might need an electrician. But that would mean a second wedding speech, so maybe not.

My daughter was a jeans and T-shirt sort of girl. But she's always dreamt of a fairytale wedding. And today her dream has come true. You know, Susie and Matt planned this wonderful event themselves. But the really fantastic thing is that they have planned more than their wedding – they have planned their marriage. They know where they're going, and how they're going to get there. They have planned their new life together.

I would now like to propose a toast:

Susie, my darling,
You make me so glad.
And I'll thank you forever
For calling me 'Dad'.

Susie and Matt,
My daughter and my son,
I'm so delighted that today
Your new life has begun.

Ladies and Gentlemen, please raise your glasses and join me in a toast to the bride and groom: The bride and groom!

Here is a selection of books and websites which should prove of interest and value both to fathers of the bride and their daughters.

Planning a wedding

Your Pocket Wedding Planner, Elizabeth Catherine Miles (How To Books).
How to Get Married in Green, Susan St Maur (How To Books).
Planning a Wedding Reception at Home, Carol Godsmark (How To Books).
The Complete Best Man, John Bowden (How To Books).
The DIY Wedding Manual, Lisa Sodeau (How To Books).
Wedding Secrets, Tamryn Kirby (Foulsham).

www.confetti.co.uk
www.hitched.co.uk
www.weddingguide.co.uk

Church weddings

To find all the requirements and procedures for getting married in church, see:

www.findachurch.co.uk

Civil ceremonies

If it's going to be a civil ceremony, the most informative site is:

www.registerofficeweddings.com

Approved premises

The Marriages Act 1994 has permitted civil marriages to take place outside the register office. Other venues can now be licensed to allow civil ceremonies to be performed there. There are now thousands of registered venues throughout England and Wales.

For a full list of approved premises, visit:

www.approvedpremises.co.uk

Civil partnerships

Although, legally speaking, they are not 'weddings', civil partnership ceremonies are similar to civil weddings. For more details, log on to:

www.civilpartnerships.org.uk

Specific faiths and cultures

In our multicultural society, interfaith marriages are becoming more and more common. A good general site which includes discussion on related issues is:

www.interfaithmarriage.co.uk

If you want to find out more about the beliefs and traditions of a specific faith or culture, visit the relevant site:

Hindu

www.lalwani.demon.co.uk/sonney/wedding.htm

Humanist

www.humanism.org.uk/weddings

Jewish

www.beingjewish.com.cycle/wedding.html

Mormon

www.templemarriage.com

Muslim

www.mybindi.com/weddings/ceremonies/muslim/cfm

Sikh

www.sikhs.org/wedding

Wedding suppliers

There are thousands – possibly millions – of these websites out there. The inclusion of a particular site does *not* imply recommendation. Ultimately, it's down to you and the happy couple to do a little surfing to find the most suitable ones, given your particular circumstances and requirements.

Limousine hire

www.american-limousines.co.uk (organised by UK postcode)
www.stretched-4-u.co.uk
www.callalimo.co.uk
www.limohiredirectory.com
www.limoshop.co.uk

Music

www.pnms.co.uk
www.mfiles.co.uk
www.gig-guide.co.uk
www.hiway.co.uk
www.excite.co.uk

Wedding suit hire

www.wedding-service.co.uk
www.menswear-hire.co.uk
www.countywedding.co.uk

Wedding gifts

www.thegiftexperience.co.uk
www.bust-ed.co.uk
www.shopsafe.co.uk
www.greatgifts.org
www.coolershopping.co.uk

Advice on finance

The following titles were written for an American readership. However, the basic principles expounded are equally applicable in the UK.

The Newlyweds' Guide to Investing and Personal Finance, Carol L. Coqhill (Career Press).

Yes, You Can . . . Achieve Financial Harmony: A Newlyweds' Guide to Understanding Money, Sam Goller and Deborah Shouse (Andrews McMeel Publishing).

Financial Bliss: How to Grow Wealthy Together, Sarah Pennells (Prentice Hall Life).

Get a Financial Life: Personal Finance in your Twenties and Thirties, Beth Kobliner (Fireside Press).

www.cheap-wedding-success.co.uk
www.moneysavingexpert.com
www.fool.co.uk

In addition to offering useful general financial advice for couples, each of these sites also provides imaginative money saving strategies for brides and their dads.

Making your speech

I must declare an interest on this one:

Making the Father of the Bride's Speech, John Bowden (How To Books).
Making a Wedding Speech, John Bowden (How to Books).

Index

THE STEP-BY-STEP GUIDE TO PLANNING YOUR WEDDING

Your dream wedding starts with this first simple step

LYNDA WRIGHT

Your wedding day marks the beginning of a new and exciting chapter in your life, so you'll want to make sure it's as wonderful as you always dreamed it would be.

This book will guide you through all the organisational detail of your wedding preparations so that you'll feel completely confident about the many choices and decisions you will have to make.

Written and designed in a logical, easy-to-use style, it concentrates on the practical aspects of preparing for your big day and is divided into three parts:

- The Countdown Calendar, detailing all the vital steps at each stage of the preparations.

- The Action Plans, showing the step by step sequences needed to organise the transport, flowers, photography and all the other essentials.

- The Checklists, providing lots of space for you to record all the relevant information, so that you can track your progress and ensure that nothing has been overlooked.

If you follow this book step by step, you'll feel confident that your big day will be a wonderful success and one that you'll remember for the rest of your life.

ISBN 978-1-84528-410-7

THE DIY WEDDING MANUAL

How to create your perfect day without a celebrity budget

LISA SODEAU

This book will show you that with a little bit of planning and preparation, it is possible to have the day of your dreams without starting married life in debt. It's packed with money-saving ideas for: stationery, flowers, transport, hair and make-up, photographs, food and drink, the reception and much more – including tips from real brides and over 100 budget busting ideas.

ISBN 978-1-84528-405-3

PLANNING A WEDDING

ELIZABETH CATHERINE MYERS

This book contains everything you need to know to plan a wedding. With it you will feel confident that you have all the details covered, and that everything is in place for a successful and happy day.

Ideas, checklists, tips and reminders will help make sure that you cover all the areas you need to, including the ones that are easy to miss. And you will be able to keep everything you need in one place.

- Deciding where to have the wedding
- Choosing the venue for the reception
- Organising the guest list and the seating plan
- Designing the invitations
- Choosing your colours, themes and decorations
- Arranging the entertainment
- Organising photography and videos
- Hiring the cars and managing transport

'Full of essential information, tips and ideas, and the handy task list will help make sure the preparation goes without a hitch.' Wedding Cakes

The author, Elizabeth Catherine Myers, has worked in event management for the past decade, and has been involved in organising many large-scale conferences and formal dinners. She subsequently launched a wedding planning service which specialises in providing value-for-money wedding packages for couples. She is also the author of the *The Pocket Wedding Planner*.

ISBN 978-1-84528-389-6

PLANNING A WEDDING RECEPTION AT HOME

CAROL GODSMARK

This book will enable you to plan a wedding reception at home either with or without a caterer. There's a lot to think about: hiring the marquee, making sure you have everything that you need on hand – the things you take for granted if the reception is at a hotel, such as loos, adequate electrical power, parking, a stage for the band and lots more. This book will make sure you cover everything you need so the day goes smoothly.

ISBN 978-1-84528-295-0

HOW TO GET MARRIED IN GREEN

SUZAN ST MAUR

As the whole "green" subject becomes more and more complex – combining environmental, ethical and organic issues, some of which can be conflicting – it's getting progressively harder to work out how to make your wedding eco-friendly without ending up with a glorified mudbath. Yet, quite rightly, many couples now want their weddings designed to help keep our planet, environment, agriculture and employment ethics as healthy as possible . . . without compromising on style, glamour, quality and, of course, fun. In this book Suzan St Maur neatly unravels the increasingly tangled web of green issues relating to weddings; so that you can enjoy your wedding (and its planning) even more, because you know you're making a difference.

ISBN 978-1-84528-270-7

WEDDING SPEECHES FOR WOMEN

SUZAN ST MAUR

'It's no longer just the men who get to speak at weddings – here's help for female speakers to plan their timing and content including jokes, poems and quotations.' – Pure Weddings

'The perfect gift for those special people who have agreed to be part of your special day.' Wedding Dresses

ISBN 978-1-84528-107-6

THE COMPLETE BEST MAN

JOHN BOWDEN

'A valuable asset for the friend who didn't realise quite how much is involved in being his mate's best man!' – Wedding Dresses

'A lifesaver for a terrified best man.' – Pure Weddings

This handbook will show you how to become the perfect best man . . . a best man who knows how to combine the best of the old with the best of the new.

ISBN 978-1-84528-104-5

BE THE BEST, BEST MAN & MAKE A STUNNING SPEECH

PHILLIP KHAN-PANNI

'Essential reading, and a great gift for those preparing to stand and deliver on the big day.' – Wedding Day

'Gives you all the low down on how to go about delivering a speech that will hold and impress the audience . . . also contains all the etiquette and do's and don'ts for the wedding as well as tips on helping to calm nerves.' – For the Bride

ISBN 978-1-85703-802-6

MAKING THE BEST MAN'S SPEECH

JOHN BOWDEN

The essential handbook for every petrified best man. It reveals how to prepare and present a unique and memorable best man's speech, explains how to conquer nerves and gives you plenty of sample speeches, jokes and one-liners to make your best man's speech sparkle like vintage champagne.

ISBN 978-1-85703-659-6

MAKING THE BRIDEGROOM'S SPEECH

JOHN BOWDEN

This handy guide gives the bridegroom all the tools you need to make a brilliant, humorous, but sincere speech. The author, a professional speaker with over 20 years experience supplies a rich selection of stories, jokes and quotations which can be easily adapted.

ISBN 978-1-85703-567-4

How To Books are available through all good bookshops, or you can order direct from us through Grantham Book Services.

Tel: +44 (0)1476 541080
Fax: +44 (0)1476 541061
Email: *orders@gbs.tbs-ltd.co.uk*

Or via our website
www.howtobooks.co.uk

To order via any of these methods please quote the title(s) of the book(s) and your credit card number together with its expiry date.

For further information about our books and catalogue, please contact:

How To Books
Spring Hill House
Spring Hill Road
Begbroke, Oxford OX5 1RX

Visit our web site at
www.howtobooks.co.uk

Or you can contact us by email at *info@howtobooks.co.uk*